O9-ABG-279

Santillana

Spotlight

on English

NO LONGER
the property of
Whitaker Library

Academic English for success in content and literacy

ASSESSMENTS TEACHER'S MANUAL

© 2008 Santillana USA Publishing Company, Inc.
All rights reserved. No part of this book may be reproduced
or transmitted in any form or by any means, electronic
or mechanical, including photocopying, recording or by any
information storage and retrieval system, without permission
in writing from the publisher.

Published in the United States of America.

Santillana Spotlight on English Assessments
Teacher's Manual Level 5
ISBN10: 1-60396-138-0
ISBN13: 978-1-60396-138-7

Editorial Staff
Editorial Director: Mario Castro
Contributing Writers: Stephan L. Jackson & Associates
Developmental Editor: Patricia E. Acosta
Design and Production Manager: Mónica R. Candelas Torres
Design and Layout: Mauricio Laluz
Cover Design and Layout: Studio Montage
Cover Illustration or Photograph: © Rachel Royse / Corbis
Illustrations: Santillana USA

Santillana USA Publishing Company, Inc.
2105 NW 86th Avenue, Miami FL 33122

Printed in Colombia by Quebecor World Bogotá

12 11 10 09 08   1 2 3 4 5 6 7 8 9 10

Contents

Introduction

The **Santillana Spotlight on English Assessments** system is an integral part of the **Santillana Spotlight on English** program, designed to help nonnative English-speakers become more proficient in the English language.

Separate Domains Assessments

The Separate Domains Assessments provide information about English proficiency for each student through all the units in this program. Additionally, the system includes a Pre-Assessment for initial assessment and a Post-Assessment for year-end evaluation. These results give teachers, administrators, parents, and students a comprehensive overview of how the students are performing at different stages of the English-language acquisition process. Each Unit Assessment provides information on both general language development and specific skills in the areas of listening, reading, writing, and speaking. This information can be used to focus instruction where it will have the most impact.

The *Spotlight on English Assessments* system allows teachers to group students for targeted and generalized instruction, inspect ongoing language development, adjust instruction based on students' needs and abilities, and reflect on student performance at the end of the year.

The Listening, Reading, and Writing assessments are administered to groups of students, while the Speaking assessments are administered individually. The Administration section of this manual (pages X–XIV) and the annotations on each page walk the examiner through each step of the assessment administration process, indicating directions and appropriate prompts.

Once administration is complete, the scoring process is described on pages XVII–XXXIV of this manual. Also included are answer keys for multiple-choice items and rubrics for scoring constructed-response items (pages XXI–XXVII), along with several example responses for every possible score.

Each component of the Unit Assessments (Listening, Reading, Writing, and Speaking) is scored on a 20-point scale, while the Pre- and Post-Assessments are scored on a 30-point scale. Once this score has been determined using the answer key and rubrics, it can easily be converted to one of three levels: Beginning, Intermediate, and Advanced. These assessments are specific to the content taught in *Spotlight*. They are not designed to compare a student, or group of students, with a general population, such as a state or the nation. Results show student performance within the context of the *Spotlight* instruction initially, over time, and at year's end.

Separate Domains Assessments System at a Glance

- Assessments measure general language development and specific skills in the areas of listening, reading, writing, and speaking.

- All components of the Unit Assessments are scored on a 20-point scale, while the Pre- and Post-Assessments are scored on a 30-point scale.

- Scores are easily converted to one of three levels: Beginning, Intermediate, and Advanced. They can also be converted to one of five levels: Beginning, Early Intermediate, Intermediate, Early Advanced, and Advanced.

Integrated Domains Assessments

Besides the more structured assessments, *Spotlight* includes rubrics and forms for rating student performance in the classroom during the course of regular instruction.

The Integrated Domains Assessments let teachers structure their observations of students as they work on activities and solve problems with their peers. As students are involved in each activity, the examiner observes their interactions and written samples, using the individual observation forms provided to take notes and record student performance. These forms and rubrics allow instructors to evaluate students in an environment that more closely reflects how language is actually used to communicate.

When using this method, teachers can rate students in two domains of language: Comprehension and Production. The Comprehension rubric rates each student's listening and reading skills, while the Production rubric is used to rate each student's speaking and writing skills.

The recommended activities for these kinds of assessments are indicated in the Teacher's Guide with this icon. Teachers, however, may use these rubrics with other activities when it is more convenient to do so. It is recommended that teachers review the Integrated Domains rubrics on pages XXIX–XXXIII before using the Integrated Domains Assessment forms.

Integrated Domains Assessments at a Glance

- The Integrated Domains Assessments allow teachers to structure their observations of students as they work on activities and solve problems with their peers.

- The recommended activities for these kinds of assessments are indicated in the Teacher's Manual with this icon:

- The Comprehension rubrics are provided to rate the student's listening and reading skills, while the Production rubrics are used to rate the student's speaking and writing skills.

Administration Procedures

The *Spotlight Assessments* system contains assessments covering each of the eight instructional units, as well as a Pre-Assessment for use when students enter the program, and a Post-Assessment to be used at the end of the school year.

The assessments are divided into the four language domains: Listening, Reading, Writing, and Speaking. The Listening, Reading, and Writing assessments are designed to be given to groups of students, while the Speaking section is administered individually. Administration of these assessments requires the examiner to set aside time during the school day to assess students using a tightly controlled and scripted method. The tests are not timed, but administering all parts of a Unit Assessment to a group of 20 students typically takes about two hours.

Examiners should review the administration procedures below, and then follow the scripted administration instructions provided in this manual.

General Preparation

To ensure an accurate measure of language proficiency, examiners should carefully plan the assessment administration. Examiners should be fluent in English, and should have read and understood this manual, including all scoring rubrics (beginning on page XXI). Examiners should also carefully plan testing schedules and location for the Separate Domains Assessments.

Administering the Assessments

Depending on the subtests chosen, examiners should give all group-administered sections at once, and schedule time to pull students aside separately for the Speaking section. This section is given to individual students so that the examiner can listen closely to what the student is saying and accurately record the speech sample.

In the Unit Assessments, each section of the assessment (except Writing) is divided into three parts–Part A, Part B, and Part C. Parts B and C contain fewer, but more difficult, items than Part A. In the Pre- and Post-Assessments, an additional part is added to the Speaking section. This section includes a story-retelling item, which offers a more complete assessment of students' speaking abilities at the beginning and end of the year. Each part is described below, along with notes on administration.

Listening   This section of the assessment requires that students demonstrate comprehension of simple nouns and brief narratives. In the Unit Assessments, Part A consists of four multiple-choice items. For each of these items, the examiner asks students to circle an image.

Directions: *"Circle the picture of a bird."*

Part B consists of a brief narrative, which the examiner reads to the group once, followed by three multiple-choice questions relating to the narrative.

Directions: *"Who is the story about? Circle the picture."*

Part C consists of two questions about the narrative introduced in Part B. These questions are at a higher level than those in Part B, and may ask the student to make inferences from the story. The examiner reads each question and four possible responses to students, who circle the letter (a, b, c, or d) corresponding to the response that they think is correct.

In the Pre- and Post-Assessments, the items are structured in the same way, but there are seven items in Part A, four items in Part B, and three items in Part C.

Reading This section of the assessment asks students to identify the word missing from a sentence, and to answer questions about a brief narrative, which each student reads independently.

Part A consists of four multiple-choice items in the Unit Assessments, and seven items in the Pre- and Post-Assessments. For each of these items, the student is presented with a sentence that is missing a word. The student is then asked to circle the word that correctly completes the sentence.

Directions: *"Look at the sentences. A word is missing from each one. Circle the word that completes the sentence."*

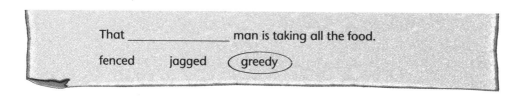

That _____ man is taking all the food.

fenced   jagged   greedy

Part B presents a narrative with three multiple-choice items in the Unit Assessments, and four items in the Pre- and Post-Assessments. Each item is a question about the story. Students are asked to choose the correct response to the question.

Directions: *"Read the story. Then, you will answer some questions about it."*

Who is the story about?

a.   The army doctor
b.   The American army
c.   Deborah Sampson
d.   George Washington

Part C consists of two questions in the Unit Assessments, and three questions in the Pre- and Post-Assessments. These questions are also about the narrative in Part B, but the questions are at a higher level, and may ask the student to make inferences from the story. Otherwise they follow the same format as the questions in Part B.

Writing This section of the assessment asks students to complete sentences based on sentence-starters, and then to write a three-paragraph passage based on a prompt.

Part A consists of four items in the Unit Assessments, and nine items in the Pre- and Post-Assessments. For each of these items, the student is presented with the beginning of a sentence and is asked to complete it.

Directions: *"Look at the example. It is the beginning of a sentence. You will write the rest of the sentence. You can write anything that makes sense to you, as long as it completes the sentence."*

The cold front ___blew in last night_____.

Part B presents the students with a topic or theme to develop. Students are expected to write three paragraphs with at least three sentences each. Students may receive partial credit for writing words or individual sentences related to the prompt, according to the scoring rubric on page XXII.

Directions: *"Use the blank lines to write three paragraphs. Each paragraph should be at least three sentences long. Remember to use capital letters and end punctuation."*

"Write three paragraphs about a natural or human-made wonder of the world."

Speaking In the Unit Assessments, this section asks a student to name three things in a picture, to describe something in that picture, and to make inferences about the picture. The student will not need anything for this assessment, but the examiner will need the *Spotlight on English* Student Book, this manual, and a copy of the Speech Observation Form (page XXXVII) for recording responses.

The examiner begins by presenting the student with a picture, or pictures, from the *Spotlight on English* Student Book. (In the Pre- and Post-Assessments, the examiner uses the images provided on pages XXXVIII and XXXIX of this manual.) The examiner asks the student to name three things in the picture(s). If the student is able to name at least one item, the examiner then asks the student to explain or describe something in the picture(s). If the student is able to answer the question, the examiner completes the assessment by asking the student to make inferences about the picture.

In the Pre- and Post-Assessments, an additional section is included in the test. In this section, the examiner reads a story to the student. After reading the story, the examiner asks the student to retell the story, taking notes on the student's version of the narrative.

Directions: *"I'm going to tell you a story. Then, I want you to tell me the same story"*

> *John wanted to plant a flower. First, he made a hole in the soil. Next, he put a seed into the hole. Then, he filled the hole with soil. But he wasn't done yet. He had to water the seed every day. For many days, John waited to see the flower. Then, one day he went out to water the plant, and he saw two tiny leaves coming up out of the soil. John kept watering the plant every day. Every day the plant got taller, the stem got thicker, and the leaves grew. Soon the flower started to grow at the top. Then, one day, when John went out to water his flower, the petals had opened. It was beautiful! John was so happy that he had cared for his plant and had waited patiently for the flower to bloom.*

"Now you tell me the story."

A Speech Observation Form is included in the Forms section (pages XL and XLI) to facilitate the process of recording responses. It is important that examiners keep a detailed record of students' responses to the items in order to complete the scoring process. Examiners should become familiar with the scoring procedures discussed in the Scoring section (pages XIX–XXVIII) before administering these assessments.

Coaching and Prompting In all sections of the assessment, acceptable prompting is indicated in the administration script. Sample items are included to help students understand how to respond to the items in each section. Examiners should make sure that students are aware of how they are expected to respond to each item. Examiners should avoid giving students hints that could indicate the correct answer or eliminate incorrect answers, except when helping students understand example items.

The *Spotlight Assessments* are designed to help teachers evaluate their students' language development throughout the school year. Some teachers may find that modification of the testing procedures helps accomplish this goal more effectively within their unique educational environment. These assessments are not norm-referenced, high-stakes tests. Therefore teachers may adapt the system to suit the needs of their students.

Speech Observation Form For Unit Assessments

This form is used to assess the Speaking section of the Separate Domains Assessment. Examiners should record the stimuli used for assessment. The stimuli should be written as concisely as possible (e.g., "car"). Then, examiners write the student's response to each stimulus, which will be scored later.

Speech Observation Form For Pre- and Post-Assessments

Because the speaking section in the Pre- and Post-Assessments is more elaborate, a different form is used to take notes on student responses to these two assessments. The three stimuli used for the assessment are provided as images on separate sheets (pages XXXVIII and XXXIX) that accompany the Speech Observation Forms. The words for the stimuli are written on the form, so examiners need only write the student's response to each question, which will be scored later. Examiners ask the first question for each of the three images. If the student responds appropriately, the examiner asks question 2, and (if the student's response is appropriate) the examiner finishes the assessment by asking question 3 (see page XIII of the Administration section). Note that there is one form for the Pre-Assessment, and another for the Post-Assessment.

Individual Student Record

This form is used to keep track of each student's performance on the *Spotlight Assessments* during the course of the school year. Every score produced by the system can be recorded here, from the Pre-Assessment, the Unit Assessments, and the Post-Assessment. For the Separate Domains Assessment, raw scores as well as levels can be tracked. It is advisable to make copies of the Individual Student Record for each student at the beginning of the year, and to record his or her performance as soon as the scoring is complete for each unit. Using this form, teachers, parents, and administrators can see where a student is having trouble and how much progress he or she is making.

Class Record

This form is used to record the performance of the entire class for a single unit of *Spotlight*. Unlike the Individual Student Record, this form provides space for writing the performance level of each student in each area tested, but does not allow for raw scores to be recorded. Therefore it is used for grouping students by proficiency level, but it does not show progress or allow for the same kind of fine-grained analysis as raw scores. It is recommended that teachers keep a copy of this form on file for each completed unit of *Spotlight*.

Integrated Domains Assessment Form

This form is used for assessing student performance on the Integrated Domains Assessment. While students are working on the assigned activity, examiners observe their interactions and takes simple notes, using the examples included with the Integrated Domains Rubrics as models. If examiners are comfortable with the rubric, they may score student performance while observing. Otherwise it is preferable to wait until after the activity to carefully review the rubrics and reflect on student performance. Examiners rate each student on Comprehension and Production, giving a score of Beginning, Intermediate, or Advanced for each area.

Portfolios

The *Spotlight Assessment* system provides a comprehensive, content-based approach to documenting student English-language skills throughout the school year. The Pre-Assessment, Unit Assessments, and Post-Assessment may be organized into a portfolio. Ideally, each student's portfolio would include all the tests completed by the student at any time during the school year, arranged chronologically. This way, teachers may, at any time, use the portfolio to show a student's progress, including speech samples and writing samples.

Pre-Assessment

A Read the following directions to the group:

I'm going to ask you to draw a circle around one of the pictures.

*Let's do the **example**. Circle the picture of a book.*

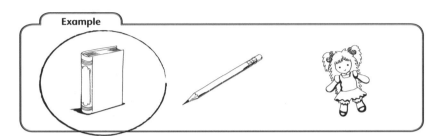

Be sure students circle the correct answer.

*Look at number **one**. Circle the picture of a bird.*

1.

*Look at number **two**. Circle the picture of a face.*

2.

*Look at number **three**. Circle the picture of a soldier.*

3.

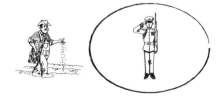

*Look at number **four**. Circle the picture of* something with a ribbon.

*Look at number **five**. Circle the picture of a* protest.

*Look at number **six**. Circle the picture of a* lumberjack.

*Look at number **seven**. Circle the picture of a* cemetery.

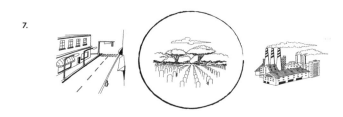

B Read the following directions to the group:

I will read a story. Then, you will answer some questions about it by circling the correct picture. Now listen to the story.

> Jim is a farmer who grows wheat. His farm is important because his wheat is used to make bread for people all over the country. It is also used to make many other foods. Wheat is one of the most important grains. Jim's farm also produces bales of hay to sell to other farms. But Jim is very worried this year. There is a drought that could hurt his crops. Even though he has a good irrigation system, there is not enough water for his crops. Jim goes to sleep every night hoping for rain. Then, one night while Jim is sleeping, a storm comes in. He wakes up to the sound of thunder in the distance. Jim gets out of bed and looks outside. He sees huge clouds blowing in from the north. It rains all night, and all the next day. It rains all week. Jim's crops become strong and healthy. After two weeks of rain, the clouds start to thin, and the sun comes out. It looks like Jim will have a good harvest after all.

Let's do the **example***. Who is the story about? Circle the picture.*

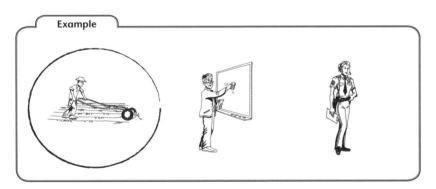
Example

Observe students completing the example and assist them as necessary. Then, say:

The story is about Jim, who is a farmer. Did you circle the picture of the farmer? That is the answer.

Let's do number **eight***. What does Jim grow on his farm? Circle the picture.*

8.

Look at number **nine**. *Where is Jim when he hears the storm? Circle the picture.*

9.

Look at number **ten**. *What does Jim sell to other farms? Circle the picture.*

10.
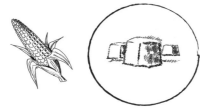

Look at number **eleven**. *What is made from wheat? Circle the picture.*

11.

C Read the following directions to the group:

*Now I'm going to ask you some more questions about the story. For each question,
I'll read four answers. Circle the letter of the correct answer.*

*Let's do the **example**. What does Jim hope for?*

*If Jim hopes for **an irrigation system**, circle the letter **a**.*
*If Jim hopes for **a drought**, circle the letter **b**.*
*If Jim hopes for **rain**, circle the letter **c**.*
*If Jim hopes for **wind**, circle the letter **d**.*

Observe students completing the example and assist them as necessary. Then, say:

Jim hopes for rain. Did you circle the letter c? That is the answer.

Be sure students circle the correct answer.

*Let's do number **twelve**. How does the drought hurt Jim's crops?*

*If it hurts them by **keeping them dry**, circle the letter **a**.*
*If it hurts them by **flooding the land**, circle the letter **b**.*
*If it hurts them by **giving them a disease**, circle the letter **c**.*
*If it hurts them by **bringing the storm**, circle the letter **d**.*

*Let's do number **thirteen**. Why is wheat an important crop?*

*If it's because wheat **can be sold to other farms**, circle the letter **a**.*
*If it's because wheat **does not need much water**, circle the letter **b**.*
*If it's because wheat **is used to make many foods**, circle the letter **c**.*
*If it's because wheat **is made from bread**, circle the letter **d**.*

*Let's do number **fourteen**. Why does Jim have an irrigation system?*

*If he has it to **eat the crops**, circle the letter **a**.*
*If he has it to **sell hay to other farms**, circle the letter **b**.*
*If he has it to **harvest the crops**, circle the letter **c**.*
*If he has it to **water the crops**, circle the letter **d**.*

A Read the following directions to the group:

Look at the sentences. A word is missing from each one. Circle the word that completes the sentence.

Now do the **example**.

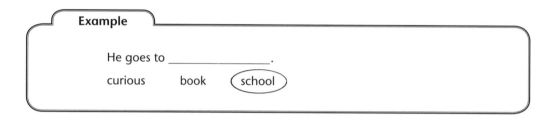

Example

He goes to _____.

curious   book   ⟨school⟩

Observe students completing the example and assist them as necessary. Then, say:

Did you circle the third word, school? *That is the word. He goes to* school.

Be sure students circle the correct answer.

Now circle the words for numbers **one** *through* **seven**.

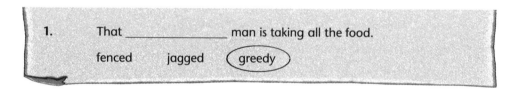

1.   That _____ man is taking all the food.

fenced   jagged   ⟨greedy⟩

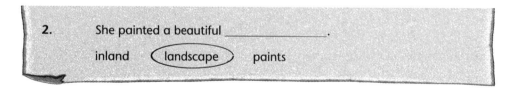

2.   She painted a beautiful _____.

inland   ⟨landscape⟩   paints

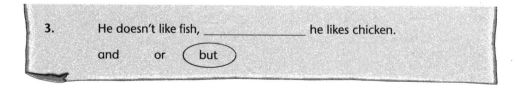

3.   He doesn't like fish, _____ he likes chicken.

and   or   ⟨but⟩

4. He would not go outside because the storm was so _____.

(scary)   shallow   sizzling

5. She was the only student who _____ the problem.

(solved)   lashed   smiled

6. The tornado will _____ our new house.

destroys   destroyed   (destroy)

7. He used the _____ to find his way back to land.

figurehead   (compass)   college

B Read the following directions to the group:

Read the story. Then, you will answer some questions about it. For every question, circle the correct answer.

> Deborah Sampson was a legendary woman who fought in the American army. When the Americans were fighting the British, many women helped. Some of them worked as nurses, and some of them spied on the British. Women were not allowed to fight in battles. Deborah wanted to fight as a soldier, so she dressed up like a man and enlisted in the army. She was in the army for three years and fought in several battles, until she got a disease. When she went to see the army doctor, he discovered that she was a woman. She had to leave the army, but she is a legend to this day for her loyalty and courage. In fact, there is a statue of her in front of the library in her hometown.

When students have finished reading, ask them to answer the example question.

Example

Who is the story about?

  a.   The army doctor

  b.   The American army

  (c.) Deborah Sampson

  d.   George Washington

Once students have answered the example question, say:

Did you circle the third answer, "Deborah Sampson"? That is the correct answer. The story is about Deborah Sampson. Now answer questions **eight** *through* **fourteen**.

8.   Whom did Deborah want to fight against?

  (a.) The British

  b.   The American army

  c.   The army doctor

  d.   The American soldiers

9.   How was Deborah able to enlist in the army?

   a.   She pretended to be a doctor.

   b.   She pretended to be a British soldier.

   (c.) She pretended to be a man.

   d.   She pretended to be a spy.

10.   When did Deborah go to see the doctor?

   a.   When she enlisted in the army

   (b.) When she got a disease

   c.   When she became a nurse

   d.   When she left the army

11.   What did the doctor discover about Deborah?

   a.   That she was a soldier

   b.   That she had a disease

   (c.) That she was a man

   d.   That she was in the army

C Allow students additional time to answer questions twelve through fourteen.

12.   Why did some women work as nurses and spies?

   a.   Because they wanted to help, but were afraid to fight

   (b.)   Because they wanted to help, but weren't allowed to fight

   c.   Because they could not think of a way to help

   d.   Because they liked the nurse's uniform

13.   Why did Deborah have to leave the army?

   a.   Because she was sick

   b.   Because she wanted to become a nurse

   c.   Because she didn't like the doctor

   (d.)   Because she was a woman

14.   Why is there a statue of Deborah in front of the library?

   a.   Because she got a disease in the library

   b.   Because she enlisted in the army at the library

   c.   To remind women not to join the army

   (d.)   To honor her loyalty and courage

A Read the following directions to the group:

Look at the example. It is the beginning of a sentence. You will write the rest of the sentence. You can write anything that makes sense to you, as long as it completes the sentence.

Now do the **example**.

> **Example**
>
> I like to _____
>
> _____.

Observe students completing the example and assist them as necessary. Then, say:

Did you write something that you like to do? One answer could be "play games." The sentence would be "I like to play games."

Be sure students understand the directions.

Now finish the sentences for numbers **one** *through* **nine**.

1. The cold front _____

   _____.

2. Her mom encourages her _____

   _____.

3. The rhythm of the _____

   _____.

4. This is a risky _____

   _____.

5. His siblings _____

_____ .

6. I used the scale to _____

_____ .

7. A myth _____

_____ .

8. There are pests _____

_____ .

9. Our solar system _____

_____ .

B Read the following directions to the group:

You will use the blank lines to write three paragraphs. Each paragraph should be at least three sentences long. Remember to use capital letters and end punctuation.

Now look at the **example**. *There are three paragraphs describing life on a farm. The first paragraph is about the land that the farm is on, and says* "Our farm is very big. It goes as far as you can see. The land is very flat, and there are no rivers or lakes nearby. On one side, there is a forest. On the other sides, there are more farms."

The second paragraph is about the crops and animals on the farm, and says "We grow mostly corn on our farm. We have huge fields of corn. We also raise cattle on the farm. We have fields of grass for the cattle to eat. They go out to the fields in the morning, and we bring them back in the evening."

The third paragraph is about the work on the farm, and says "It takes a lot of work to run the farm. We have to get up very early to milk the cows. We have to milk them before breakfast. We plant the corn in the spring. That is a lot of work. Then, in the fall we have to harvest it. In the summer we have to make sure the corn has water. The farm is a lot of work, but we enjoy it."

Example. Write three paragraphs describing life on a farm.

> Our farm is very big. It goes as far as you can see. The land is very flat, and there are no rivers or lakes nearby. On one side, there is a forest. On the other sides, there are more farms.
>
> We grow mostly corn on our farm. We have huge fields of corn. We also raise cattle on the farm. We have fields of grass for the cattle to eat. They go out to the fields in the morning, and we bring them back in the evening.
>
> It takes a lot of work to run the farm. We have to get up very early to milk the cows. We have to milk them before breakfast. We plant the corn in the spring. That is a lot of work. Then, in the fall we have to harvest it. In the summer we have to make sure the corn has water. The farm is a lot of work, but we enjoy it.

Now look at number **ten**. *Use the blank lines on both sides of the page to write three paragraphs describing the weather where you live, the clothes you wear, and the activities you do in that weather.*

10. Write three paragraphs describing the weather where you live, the clothes you wear, and the activities you do in that weather.

Administer this assessment individually. Use the Speech Observation Form (Pre-Assessment) to record all responses to the questions below.

A Using a copy of the Pre-Assessment Images for Speaking (provided at the back of this manual, in the Forms section), ask the student to name each of the images.

1. *What's this?* (Point to a picture.)

Repeat this question for all three images. If the student responds in a language other than English, ask the student to respond in English (*Can you say it in English?*). If the student cannot name at least one item in English, stop and do not ask the rest of the questions.

B Ask the student to explain or describe something about the pictures (in this example, a *kitchen*).

2. *What's a kitchen for?* (or *What do you do in a kitchen?*)

If the student gives a plausible but incorrect response, rephrase the question or ask the student for alternative responses. For instance, if you ask *What do you do in a kitchen?* and the student replies *I go there*, you may ask the student what he or she does after going to the kitchen. If the student is unable to answer, stop and do not ask question 3.

C Ask the student to explain why the function of the item is important.

3. *Why is it important to cook food?* (or *Why do we need to cook food?*)

If the student responds with a description of the function, ask the question using his or her description. For instance, if the student says *To make lunch*, ask why we need to make lunch.

D In this section, prompt the student to repeat the story below. Take notes about the student's version of the story as he or she is telling it.

I'm going to tell you a story. Then, I want you to tell me the same story.

> *John wanted to plant a flower. First, he made a hole in the soil. Next, he put a seed into the hole. Then, he filled the hole with soil. But he wasn't done yet. He had to water the seed every day. For many days, John waited to see the flower. Then, one day he went out to water the plant, and he saw two tiny leaves coming up out of the soil. John kept watering the plant every day. Every day the plant got taller, the stem got thicker, and the leaves grew. Soon the flower started to grow at the top. Then, one day, when John went out to water his flower, the petals had opened. It was beautiful! John was so happy that he had cared for his plant and had waited patiently for the flower to bloom.*

Now you tell me the story.

A Read the following directions to the group:

I'm going to ask you to draw a circle around one of the pictures.

*Let's do the **example**. Circle the picture of rain.*

Be sure students circle the correct answer.

*Look at number **one**. Circle the picture of a tornado.*

1.

*Look at number **two**. Circle the picture of a cloud.*

2.

*Look at number **three**. Circle the picture of precipitation.*

3.

*Look at number **four**. Circle the picture of lightning.*

4.

B Read the following directions to the group:

I will read a story. Then, you will answer some questions about it by circling the correct picture. Now listen to the story.

> The Mendoza family works very hard to protect their apple orchard from damaging weather events. To know what the weather will be like, the family watches the weather forecast on TV. During spring, they watch for thunderstorms. Thunderstorms bring heavy rain, so the family needs to protect their orchard from flooding. During winter, they watch for blizzards. Blizzards bring heavy snowfall, so the family needs to protect their orchard from freezing. During summer, they watch for periods of drought. When there is a drought, there isn't much water available, so the family needs to protect the orchard from drying out. Weather can surely affect an apple orchard!

*Let's do the **example**. What fruit does the family grow in their orchard? Circle the picture.*

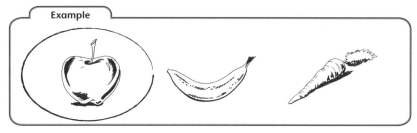

Observe students completing the example and assist them as necessary. Then, say:

The family grows apples in their orchard. Did you circle the picture of the apple? That is the answer.

*Let's do number **five**. What weather event can cause flooding?*

5.

*Let's do number **six**. What weather event can cause an orchard to freeze?*

6.

*Let's do number **seven**. What does the family watch on TV?*

7.

c Read the following directions to the group:

Now I'm going to ask you some more questions about the story. For each question, I'll read four answers. Circle the letter of the correct answer.

*Let's do the **example**. What happens during a thunderstorm?*

*If there is **a blizzard**, circle the letter **a**.*

*If there is **lightning and heavy rain**, circle the letter **b**.*

*If there is **a drought and no rain**, circle the letter **c**.*

*If there is **cold wind and snow**, circle the letter **d**.*

Observe students completing the example and assist them as necessary. Then, say:

There is lightning and heavy rain during a thunderstorm. Did you circle the letter b? *That is the answer.*

*Let's do number **eight**. Why does the family watch the weather forecast on TV?*

*If it's so they can **be prepared for severe weather events**, circle the letter **a**.*

*If it's so they can **hear the news of the day**, circle the letter **b**.*

*If it's so they can **find out what is going on around the country**, circle the letter **c**.*

*If it's so they can **learn more about the types of clouds**, circle the letter **d**.*

*Let's do number **nine**. Why does the family need to protect the orchard when there's a drought?*

*If it's because **there is too much snow,** circle the letter **a**.*

*If it's because **there isn't enough wind**, circle the letter **b**.*

*If it's because **there is too much rain**, circle the letter **c**.*

*If it's because **there isn't enough rain**, circle the letter **d**.*

A Read the following directions to the group:

Look at the sentences. A word is missing from each one. Circle the word that completes the sentence.

Now do the **example**.

> **Example**
>
> There are many types of _____ in the sky.
>
> (clouds)   forecasts   floods

Observe students completing the example and assist them as necessary. Then, say:

Did you circle the first word, clouds? *That is the correct word. There are many types of* clouds *in the sky.*

Now circle the words for numbers **one** *through* **four**.

1. During the thunderstorm, _____ winds damaged many trees.

   shimmering   (gusty)   jagged

2. The main _____ in the narrative is afraid of thunder.

   (character)   setting   plot

3. _____ clouds are thin and wispy.

   Hurricane   Tornado   (Cirrus)

4. The refinery was destroyed, so the _____ of oil products decreased.

   scarcity   (supply)   fragment

B Read the following directions to the group:

Read the story. Then, you will answer some questions about it. For each question, circle the correct answer.

> John's class is studying the weather. John is interested in clouds. He decides to study how different weather events are related to different types of clouds. First, he sees some cirrus clouds. These clouds are thin and very high in the sky. John notices that the weather is pleasant when he sees these clouds. A few days later, John sees some cumulonimbus clouds. These clouds are gray and very tall. He notices that the weather is stormy when he sees these clouds. He also notices that these clouds can produce heavy rain, hail, and lightning. Then, John writes a report about his observations and presents it to the class. John and his classmates wish they could see some cirrus clouds today!

When students have finished reading, ask them to answer the example question.

Example

What is John's class studying?

- **a.** The weather
- **b.** The forecast
- **c.** Sunny days
- **d.** Rainy days

Once students have answered the example question, say:

Did you circle the first answer, "The weather"? That is the correct answer. John's class is studying the weather. Now answer questions ***five*** *through* ***nine***.

5.   What is John interested in?

- **a.** Rain
- **b.** Hail
- **c.** Clouds
- **d.** Storms

6. What does John decide to study?

    a. How clouds produce rain

    b. Why some types of clouds look prettier than others

    c. What are the best kinds of clouds

    (d.) How different weather events are related to different types of clouds

7. What clouds are thin and high in the sky?

    (a.) Cirrus

    b. Cumulus

    c. Stratus

    d. Cumulonimbus

C Allow students additional time to answer questions eight and nine.

8. What kind of clouds are you likely to see on a stormy day?

    a. Cirrus clouds

    (b.) Cumulonimbus clouds

    c. Hail

    d. Lightning

9. Why do you think John and his classmates wish they could see some cirrus clouds?

    a. Because they want to see if John's observations are right

    b. Because they want to write a new report

    c. Because they want to see the rain

    (d.) Because they want to have pleasant weather

A Read the following directions to the group:

Look at the example. It is the beginning of a sentence. You will write the rest of the sentence. You can write anything that makes sense to you, as long as it completes the sentence.

*Now do the **example**.*

Example

Weather _____

_____.

Observe students completing the example and assist them as necessary. Then, say:

Did you write something about the weather? One answer could be "affects everyone." The sentence would be "Weather affects everyone."

Be sure students understand the directions.

*Now finish the sentences for numbers **one** through **four**.*

1. A tornado is _____

   _____.

2. Hurricanes can _____

   _____.

3. The drought caused _____

   _____.

4. The soil _____

   _____.

B Read the following directions to the group:

You will use the blank lines to write three paragraphs. Each paragraph should be at least three sentences long. Remember to use capital letters and end punctuation.

Now look at the **example**. *There are three paragraphs telling a story about a real weather event and real people. The first paragraph describes the setting of the story and introduces the characters, and says* "There is a part of the state of Texas known as the Texas panhandle. It is called the panhandle because the northern part of the state actually looks like the handle of a pan. That part of the state often has severe weather. When Sheila was a young girl, she and her family moved to the Texas panhandle."

The second paragraph tells about the characters and the events in the story, and says "Sheila and her family had to get used to the stormy weather. One afternoon, there was a severe weather warning on TV. The announcer told everyone to take cover because a tornado was nearby. Soon after the warning, the sky filled with dark cumulus storm clouds. Sheila and her family ran to a tornado shelter."

The third paragraph tells how the characters solved the problem in the story, and says "They all went into the shelter as the tornado hit. It sounded like a train! When they came out of the shelter, they were amazed at the damage the tornado had caused. Sheila was glad that her family was safe."

Example. Write three paragraphs that tell a story about a weather event.

> There is a part of the state of Texas known as the Texas panhandle. It is called the panhandle because the northern part of the state actually looks like the handle of a pan. That part of the state often has severe weather. When Sheila was a young girl, she and her family moved to the Texas panhandle.
>
> Sheila and her family had to get used to the stormy weather. One afternoon, there was a severe weather warning on TV. The announcer told everyone to take cover because a tornado was nearby. Soon after the warning, the sky filled with dark cumulus storm clouds. Sheila and her family ran to a tornado shelter.
>
> They all went into the shelter as the tornado hit. It sounded like a train! When they came out of the shelter, they were amazed at the damage the tornado had caused. Sheila was glad that her family was safe.

Now look at number ***five***. *Use the blank lines to write three paragraphs that tell a real or made-up story about a weather event.*

5. Write three paragraphs that tell a real or made-up story about a weather event.

Administer this assessment individually. Use the Speech Observation Form to record all responses.

A Direct the student's attention to the pictures on pages 10 and 11 in the Student Book. Use the pictures to elicit a verbal response from the student. Say:

Look at these pictures. I will ask you to talk about them.

1. *Point to and name three things in the pictures.*

If the student responds in a language other than English, ask the student to respond in English (*Can you say it in English?*). If the student cannot name at least one item in the pictures in English, stop and do not ask the rest of the questions.

B Ask the student to explain or describe something in one of the pictures.

2. *What's the weather like in this picture?* (Point to the picture of a flood.)

If the student gives a plausible but incorrect response, rephrase the question or ask the student for alternative responses. For instance, if the student says *Windy,* you may ask *What kind of weather event causes windy weather?* If the student is unable to answer, stop and do not ask question 3.

C Ask the student to make inferences about the pictures.

3. *Why do people need to wear different clothes for different kinds of weather?*

If the student gives a plausible but incomplete or incorrect response, rephrase the question or ask the student for alternative responses. For instance, if the student responds *They got coats,* ask why it is important to wear different clothes for different kinds of weather.

Unit 2 Wonders of the World

A Read the following directions to the group:

I'm going to ask you to draw a circle around one of the pictures.

*Let's do the **example**. Circle the picture of a pyramid.*

Be sure students circle the correct answer.

*Look at number **one**. Circle the picture of an animal with antlers.*

1.

*Look at number **two**. Circle the picture of pottery.*

2.

*Look at number **three**. Circle the picture of a landmark.*

3.

*Look at number **four**. Circle the picture of a book with an illustration.*

4.

Listening

27

B Read the following directions to the group:

I will read a story. Then, you will answer some questions about it by circling the correct picture. Now listen to the story.

> The Greeks of long ago created a list of human-made structures they would like to see. That list is now called the Seven Wonders of the Ancient World. Out of all the amazing wonders on that list, only the Pyramids of Egypt still stand. Now we have other lists of wonders of the world that include the Colosseum in Rome and Stonehenge. The Colosseum is included in the list because it was the largest amphitheater ever built in the Roman Empire. Stonehenge is also included in the list because there are many mysteries about why and how it was built. Some archaeologists and historians think that Stonehenge was used as a big calendar to keep track of the seasons, because of the way the stones are aligned in relation to the sun. I wish I could see these wonders of the world!

Let's do the **example**. *What do some people think Stonehenge was used as? Circle the picture.*

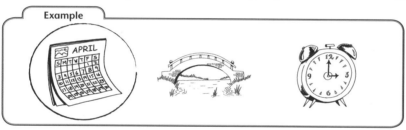

Observe students completing the example and assist them as necessary. Then, say:

Some people think that Stonehenge was used as a big calendar. Did you circle the picture of the calendar? That is the answer.

Let's do number **five**. *What Wonder of the Ancient World still stands today?*

5.

Let's do number **six**. *Who made the list of Wonders of the Ancient World?*

6.

Let's do number **seven**. *What were the stones at Stonehenge aligned with to keep track of the seasons?*

7.

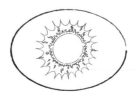

C Read the following directions to the group:

*Now I'm going to ask you some more questions about the story. For each question,
I'll read four answers. Circle the letter of the correct answer.*

*Let's do the **example**. Which one of the Seven Wonders of the Ancient World is still
standing?*

*If it is the **Pyramids of Egypt**, circle the letter **a**.*

*If it is the **Great Wall of China**, circle the letter **b**.*

*If it is the **Statue of Liberty**, circle the letter **c**.*

*If it is the **Hanging Gardens of Babylon**, circle the letter **d**.*

Observe students completing the example and assist them as necessary. Then, say:

*The ancient wonder that is still standing is the Pyramids of Egypt. Did you circle
the letter a? That is the answer.*

*Let's do number **eight**. Why was the Colosseum included in the list of wonders of the world?*

*If it's because it **was the largest amphitheater built in the Roman Empire**,
circle the letter **a**.*

*If it's because it **was made out of rocks**, circle the letter **b**.*

*If it's because it **was used as a calendar**, circle the letter **c**.*

*If it's because it **was a natural wonder of the world**, circle the letter **d**.*

*Let's do number **nine**. Why was Stonehenge included in the list of wonders of the world?*

*If it it's because it **is a tourist attraction**, circle the letter **a**.*

*If it's because it **reflects the sun**, circle the letter **b**.*

*If it's because it **the Greeks built it**, circle the letter **c**.*

*If it's because **there are many mysteries about why and how it was built**,
circle the letter **d**.*

A Read the following directions to the group:

Look at the sentences. A word is missing from each one. Circle the word that completes the sentence.

Now do the **example**.

> **Example**
>
> This is the most _____ sight I have ever seen!
>
> (wonderful)   wonder   wondered

Observe students completing the example and assist them as necessary. Then, say:

Did you circle the first word, wonderful? *That is the correct word. This is the most* wonderful *sight I have ever seen!*

Be sure students circle the correct answer.

Now circle the words for numbers **one** *through* **four**.

1.   The pieces of pottery found at Stonehenge are considered _____.
(relics)   antlers   bones

2.   I will visit the Great Pyramids, _____ I will also go to the Colosseum.
or   (and)   to

3.   These stones mark the summer and winter _____.
landmarks   slopes   (solstices)

4.   Be sure to line up the _____ points in each number.
exclamation   (decimal)   divisor

B Read the following directions to the group:

Read the story. Then, you will answer some questions about it. For each question, circle the correct answer.

> Madelyn and Jack decided to study human-made wonders of the world for their history project. First, they read stories of the wonders of the ancient world written by historians and archaeologists. After their research, they decided to focus their report on one ancient and one modern human-made structure. They chose the Pyramids of Egypt for the ancient wonder, and they picked Mount Rushmore in South Dakota for the modern one. Then, they wrote an essay about these wonders. They included illustrations of the Pyramids of Egypt and photographs of Mount Rushmore. The illustrations and the photographs both had captions. The essay had subheadings for each of the structures. After they added the title, "Two Wonders of the Ancient and Modern World," they were ready to present the essay to their class.

When students have finished reading, ask them to answer the example question.

> **Example**
>
> What title did Madelyn and Jack use for their essay?
>
> **a.** "Two Wonders of the Ancient and Modern World"
> **b.** "Wonders of the Ancient World"
> **c.** "Legendary Landmarks"
> **d.** "Pyramids of Egypt"

Once students have answered the example question, say:

*Did you circle the first answer, "Two Wonders of the Ancient and Modern World"? That is the correct answer. Madelyn and Jack used the title "Two Wonders of the Ancient and Modern World", for their essay. Now answer questions **five** through **nine**.*

5.   What did they read first?

   a.   Books written by Egyptian authors
   b.   Newspaper articles written by American reporters
   c.   Stories written by archaeologists and historians
   d.   Stories written by photographers and illustrators

6. What modern wonder of the world did Madelyn and Jack study?

    (a.) Mount Rushmore
    b. South Dakota
    c. Stonehenge
    d. Egypt

7. What type of structures did Madelyn and Jack focus on?

    a. Natural structures
    (b.) Human-made structures
    c. Granite structures
    d. Ruins

C Allow students additional time to answer questions eight and nine.

8. Why did Madelyn and Jack read stories by archaeologists and historians?

    a. Because they wanted to learn about what archaeologists and historians do
    b. Because they wanted to learn about the history of the modern world
    c. Because they could get extra credit on their report
    (d.) Because they wanted to learn about wonders of the ancient world

9. Why did Madelyn and Jack write captions?

    (a.) To describe the illustrations and the photos
    b. To describe the title of the essay
    c. To describe the subheadings of the essay
    d. To describe all the wonders of the world

A Read the following directions to the group:

Look at the example. It is the beginning of a sentence. You will write the rest of the sentence. You can write anything that makes sense to you, as long as it completes the sentence.

*Now do the **example**.*

> **Example**
>
> My favorite landmark _____
>
> _____ .

Observe students completing the example and assist them as necessary. Then, say:

Did you write about your favorite landmark? One answer could be "is Mount Rushmore in South Dakota." The sentence would be "My favorite landmark is Mount Rushmore in South Dakota."

Be sure students understand the directions.

*Now finish the sentences for numbers **one** through **four**.*

1. The antlers on the deer _____

   _____ .

2. The winter solstice _____

   _____ .

3. A compound sentence _____

   _____ .

4. Most of the rocks in the Grand Canyon _____

   _____ .

B Read the following directions to the group:

You will use the blank lines to write three paragraphs. Each paragraph should be at least three sentences long. Remember to use capital letters and end punctuation.

*Now look at the **example**. There are three paragraphs, and each paragraph informs the reader about the Great Wall of China, a human-made wonder of the world.*

The first paragraph is about the location of the wall, and says "The Great Wall of China is the world's longest structure built by people. It is more than 4,000 miles long. It runs from east to west along the northern border of China."

The second paragraph is about a description of the wall, and says "At first, the Great Wall of China was made of many walls. Then, when China was united, the emperor had the smaller walls connected. He forced more than one million people to build the wall."

The third paragraph is about the importance of the wall, and says "The Great Wall protected the country from attacks from the north. It also was a sign of the power of the Chinese Empire. Today the Great Wall of China is a popular tourist attraction. It is considered one of the greatest human-made wonders of the world."

Example. Write three paragraphs informing the reader about the Great Wall of China.

> The Great Wall of China is the world's longest structure built by people. It is more than 4,000 miles long. It runs from east to west along the northern border of China.
>
> At first, the Great Wall of China was made of many walls. Then, when China was united, the emperor had the smaller walls connected. He forced more than one million people to build the wall.
>
> The Great Wall protected the country from attacks from the north. It also was a sign of the power of the Chinese Empire. Today the Great Wall of China is a popular tourist attraction. It is considered one of the greatest human-made wonders of the world.

*Now look at number **five**. Use the blank lines to write three paragraphs informing the reader about a natural or human-made wonder of the world.*

5. Write three paragraphs informing the reader about a natural or a human-made wonder of the world.

Administer this assessment individually. Use the Speech Observation Form to record all responses.

A Direct the student's attention to the image on page 56 in the Student Book. Use the picture to elicit a verbal response from the student. Say:

Look at this picture. I will ask you to talk about it.

1. *Point to and name three things in the picture.*

If the student responds in a language other than English, ask the student to respond in English (*Can you say it in English?*). If the student cannot name at least one item in the picture in English, stop and do not ask the rest of the questions.

B Ask the student to explain or describe something in the picture.

2. *How can you tell if this is a natural or a human-made wonder?*

If the student gives a plausible but incorrect response, rephrase the question or ask the student for alternative responses. For instance, if the student says *It's made by humans,* you may ask *How can you tell that this structure was made by humans?* If the student is unable to answer, stop and do not ask question 3.

C Ask the student to make inferences about the picture.

3. *Why are some natural landmarks and some human-made structures considered wonders of the world?*

If the student gives a plausible but incomplete or incorrect response, rephrase the question or ask the student for alternative responses. For instance, if the student responds *It's important,* ask why these landmarks and structures are important enough to be considered wonders of the world.

A Read the following directions to the group:

I'm going to ask you to draw a circle around one of the pictures.

*Let's do the **example**. Circle the picture of a farm.*

Example

Be sure students circle the correct answer.

*Look at number **one**. Circle the picture of an animal with udders.*

1.

*Look at number **two**. Circle the picture of cattle.*

2.

*Look at number **three**. Circle the picture of a tractor.*

3.

*Look at number **four**. Circle the picture of a plant that has a tassel.*

4.

B Read the following directions to the group:

I will read a story. Then, you will answer some questions about it by circling the correct picture. Now listen to the story.

> *We need food to stay healthy. That is why farms are so important. Farms are where our fruits and vegetables grow. Grains to make bread also grow on farms. Our milk comes from cows that live on dairy farms. Our chicken, beef, and pork come from livestock that live on farms. The meat and produce are transported to grocery stores. There the food is displayed for the customers to buy. Most of us get our food at grocery stores. Without these foods, we would not survive, because our bodies need the nutrients to grow and be healthy.*

Let's do the **example**. *Where does food grow? Circle the picture.*

Observe students completing the example and assist them as necessary. Then, say:

Food grows on a farm. Did you circle the picture of a farm? That is the answer.

Let's do number **five**. *Where do our dairy products come from?*

5.

Let's do number **six**. *What is used to make bread?*

6.

Let's do number **seven**. *What do we need to stay healthy?*

7.

C Read the following directions to the group:

Now I'm going to ask you some more questions about the story. For each question, I'll read four answers. Circle the letter of the correct answer.

*Let's do the **example**. Where do most of us get our food?*

*If it's **at the grocery store**, circle the letter **a**.*

*If it's **on the ground**, circle the letter **b**.*

*If it's **at the dairy farm**, circle the letter **c**.*

*If it's **at the garden**, circle the letter **d**.*

Observe students completing the example and assist them as necessary. Then, say:

Most of us get our food at the grocery store. Did you circle the letter a? That is the answer.

*Let's do number **eight**. Why are farms important?*

*If it's because **our food grows there**, circle the letter **a**.*

*If it's because **animals like to live there**, circle the letter **b**.*

*If it's because **farmers need a place to rest**, circle the letter **c**.*

*If it's because **farms produce carbon dioxide**, circle the letter **d**.*

*Let's do number **nine**. Why do we need food?*

*If it's because food **makes people happy**, circle the letter **a**.*

*If it's because food **gives farmers something to do**, circle the letter **b**.*

*If it's because food **tastes good**, circle the letter **c**.*

*If it's because food **provides nutrients for our bodies**, circle the letter **d**.*

A Read the following directions to the group:

Look at the sentences. A word is missing from each one. Circle the word that best completes the sentence.

Now do the **example**.

Example

European settlers _____ with the help of Native Americans.

(survived)   urged   encouraged

Observe students completing the example and assist them as necessary. Then, say:

Did you circle the first word, survived? *That is the correct word. European settlers* survived *with the help of Native Americans.*

Be sure students circle the correct answer.

Now circle the words for numbers **one** *through* **four**.

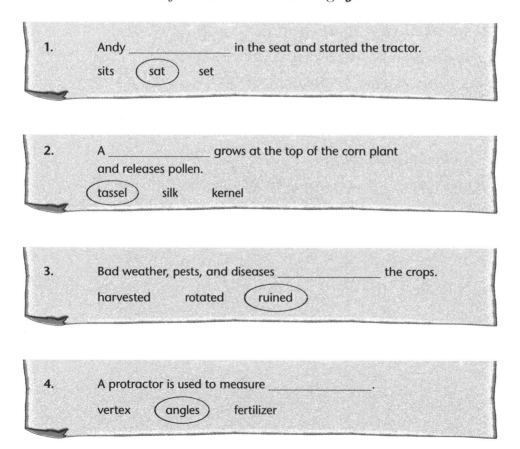

1.   Andy _____ in the seat and started the tractor.

sits   (sat)   set

2.   A _____ grows at the top of the corn plant
and releases pollen.

(tassel)   silk   kernel

3.   Bad weather, pests, and diseases _____ the crops.

harvested   rotated   (ruined)

4.   A protractor is used to measure _____.

vertex   (angles)   fertilizer

B Read the following directions to the group:

Read the story. Then, you will answer some questions about it. For each question, circle the correct answer.

> Laura lives on an organic farm. There she grows organic pumpkins. First, she plans when to plant the pumpkins and what field to use. Next, she gets manure and organic fertilizers, such as compost, and mixes them into the soil before planting the seeds. This mixture provides the soil with nutrients so that the plants can grow strong and healthy. Then, she plants the seeds, waters them, and watches them grow. This step takes the longest time. The last step happens when the pumpkins are ripe and it's time to harvest. When the pumpkins are harvested, Laura can eat the organic pumpkins, give them to friends, or sell them at the market. Also, she keeps some of the pumpkin seeds for the next year. Laura says that farming is like a circle, because every year she starts again with her pumpkin seeds and follows the same steps.

When students have finished reading, ask them to answer the example question.

Example

Where does Laura live?

(**a.**) On an organic farm

b. In a big city

c. On a citrus farm

d. On a dairy farm

Once students have answered the example question, say:

*Did you circle the first answer, "On an organic farm"? That is the correct answer. Laura lives on an organic farm. Now answer questions **five** through **nine**.*

5. What does Laura do first?

   a. She harvests the pumpkins.

   b. She fertilizes the soil.

   (**c.**) She plans where to plant the pumpkins.

   d. She buys organic foods.

6. What is compost?

   (a.) An organic fertilizer
   b. A type of soil
   c. A mixture of plants and seeds
   d. An organic pumpkin

7. What step takes the longest time?

   a. Preparing the soil
   b. Planting the seeds
   (c.) Watching the seeds grow
   d. Harvesting the pumpkins

C Allow students additional time to answer questions eight and nine.

8. Why does mixing manure and compost into the soil help the plants grow well?

   (a.) Because the mixture provides nutrients for the plants
   b. Because the mixture smells bad
   c. Because the mixture makes harvesting easier
   d. Because the mixture reduces the threat of pests

9. Why does Laura say farming is like a circle?

   a. Because pumpkins are planted in a circular field
   b. Because pumpkins are round
   c. Because circles are her favorite shape
   (d.) Because every year she starts again with her pumpkin seeds

A Read the following directions to the group:

Look at the example. It is the beginning of a sentence. You will write the rest of the sentence. You can write anything that makes sense to you, as long as it completes the sentence.

*Now do the **example**.*

> **Example**
>
> Farmers grow _____
> _____.

Observe students completing the example and assist them as necessary. Then, say:

Did you write something that farmers grow on their farms? One answer could be "crops like corn, beans, and squash." The sentence would be "Farmers grow crops like corn, beans, and squash."

Be sure students understand the directions.

*Now finish the sentences for numbers **one** through **four**.*

1. On the dairy farm _____
   _____.

2. Corn plants need _____
   _____.

3. Nutrients _____
   _____.

4. A straight angle _____
   _____.

B Read the following directions to the group:

You will use the blank lines to write three paragraphs. Each paragraph should be at least three sentences long. Remember to use capital letters and end punctuation.

Now look at the **example**. *There are three paragraphs persuading people to buy organic products.*

The first paragraph states a position, and says "To be healthy, we need to take care of our bodies by exercising and eating a balanced diet. We also need to take care of the environment by reducing pollution. When we buy organic products, we help protect both our bodies and our environment."

The second paragraph supports the position, and says "Organic products are grown without the use of harmful pesticides. Pesticides are good for getting rid of pests that ruin the crops, but they are bad for people and the environment. Pesticides pollute the soil, the water, and the foods we eat. We should not buy products from farmers that use pesticides."

The third paragraph offers solutions to the problem, and says "When we consume organic products, we help support farmers who care for our health and the environment. We also encourage other farmers to adopt responsible farming practices. Therefore we should buy organic products."

Example. Write three paragraphs persuading people to buy organic products.

> To be healthy, we need to take care of our bodies by exercising and eating a balanced diet. We also need to take care of the environment by reducing pollution. When we buy organic products, we help protect both our bodies and our environment.
>
> Organic products are grown without the use of harmful pesticides. Pesticides are good for getting rid of pests that ruin the crops, but they are bad for people and the environment. Pesticides pollute the soil, the water, and the foods we eat. We should not buy products from farmers that use pesticides.
>
> When we consume organic products, we help support farmers who care for our health and the environment. We also encourage other farmers to adopt responsible farming practices. Therefore we should buy organic products.

Now look at number **five**. *Use the blank lines to write three paragraphs persuading farmers to help protect the environment.*

5. Write three paragraphs persuading farmers to help protect the environment.

Administer this assessment individually. Use the Speech Observation Form to record all responses.

A Direct the student's attention to the image on pages 76 and 77 in the Student Book. Use the picture to elicit a verbal response from the student. Say:

Look at this picture. I will ask you to talk about it.

1. *Point to and name three things in the picture.*

If the student responds in a language other than English, ask the student to respond in English (*Can you say it in English?*). If the student cannot name at least one item in the picture in English, stop and do not ask the rest of the questions.

B Ask the student to explain or describe something in the picture.

2. *What's the farmer doing?*

If the student gives a plausible but incorrect response, rephrase the question or ask the student for alternative responses. For instance, if the student says *He working,* you may ask *What kind of work is he doing?* If the student is unable to answer, stop and do not ask question 3.

C Ask the student to make inferences about the picture.

3. *Why is the farmer putting his harvest into the barn?*

If the student gives a plausible but incomplete or incorrect response, rephrase the question or ask the student for alternative responses. For instance, if the student responds *He moving stuff,* ask why the farmer is moving his harvest into the barn.

A Read the following directions to the group:

I'm going to ask you to draw a circle around one of the pictures.

*Let's do the **example**. Circle the picture of a vegetable.*

Be sure students circle the correct answer.

*Look at number **one**. Circle the picture of the boy exercising.*

1.

*Look at number **two**. Circle the picture of a dairy product.*

2.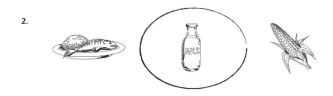

*Look at number **three**. Circle the picture of a dessert.*

3.

*Look at number **four**. Circle the picture of a refrigerator.*

4.

B Read the following directions to the group:

I will read a story. Then, you will answer some questions about it by circling the correct picture. Now listen to the story.

Betty and her family decided to improve their health. The family wanted to eat better and exercise more because they wanted to have a healthier lifestyle. They were tired of eating fast-food meals of hamburgers, french fries, and sodas. They agreed to choose healthy foods from the new food pyramid. They began their new healthy lifestyle immediately. Every day they drank milk from the dairy group. From the grain group, the family chose whole wheat bread for their sandwiches and toast. Twice a day they ate vegetables. Each day, Betty took fruit to eat with her lunch at school. The family also began exercising to burn calories so they wouldn't be overweight. Soon the whole family felt better and had more energy.

*Let's do the **example**. What was the family tired of eating? Circle the picture.*

Example

Observe students completing the example and assist them as necessary. Then, say:

The family was tired of eating fast-food meals of hamburgers, french fries, and sodas. Did you circle the picture of a hamburger, french fries, and a soda? That is the answer.

*Let's do number **five**. What is found in the grain food group?*

5.

*Let's do number **six**. What did the family eat twice a day?*

6.

*Let's do number **seven**. What did Betty eat with her lunch at school every day?*

7.

C Read the following directions to the group:

Now I'm going to ask you some more questions about the story. For each question, I'll read four answers. Circle the letter of the correct answer.

*Let's do the **example**. How did the family feel after following their new lifestyle?*

*If they **felt better and had more energy**, circle the letter **a**.*

*If they **felt stress and tension**, circle the letter **b**.*

*If they **got sick**, circle the letter **c**.*

*If they **developed high cholesterol**, circle the letter **d**.*

Observe students completing the example and assist them as necessary. Then, say:

The family felt better and had more energy. Did you circle the letter a? That is the answer.

*Let's do number **eight**. Why did the family want to eat better and exercise more?*

*If it was to **have a healthier lifestyle**, circle the letter **a**.*

*If it was to **be beautiful**, circle the letter **b**.*

*If it was to **save money on food**, circle the letter **c**.*

*If it was **to lose weight**, circle the letter **d**.*

*Let's do number **nine**. Why did the family begin exercising?*

*If it was **to be able to eat fast-food meals**, circle the letter **a**.*

*If it was **to work up an appetite to eat more food**, circle the letter **b**.*

*If it was **to get in shape to run marathons**, circle the letter **c**.*

*If it was **to burn calories so they wouldn't be overweight**, circle the letter **d**.*

A Read the following directions to the group:

Look at the sentences. A word is missing from each one. Circle the word that completes the sentence.

*Now do the **example**.*

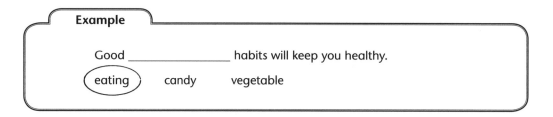

> **Example**
>
> Good _____ habits will keep you healthy.
>
> (eating)   candy   vegetable

Observe students completing the example and assist them as necessary. Then, say:

Did you circle the first word, eating? That is the correct word. Good eating habits will keep you healthy.

Be sure students circle the correct answer.

*Now circle the words for numbers **one** through **four**.*

1. Written plays are made up of _____ and stage directions.

   colon   (dialogue)   symptom

2. Soybeans are the most widely grown _____ in the world.

   (legumes)   fats   minerals

3. Too much stress can weaken the _____ system.

   immunization   immobile   (immune)

4. The _____ group helps us get calcium and vitamin D.

   cholesterol   (dairy)   nutrition

B Read the following directions to the group:

Read the story. Then, you will answer some questions about it. For each question, circle the correct answer.

> Esteban and his class have been talking about the new food pyramid. He starts thinking about what his family eats every day. He is worried that his family might not be eating a balanced diet. He tells his mom about his nutrition concerns. His mother says that she is not worried because their diet includes grains, protein and legumes, fruits and vegetables, and dairy. She points out that the soups and salads they eat daily have many vegetables in them. Then, his mother talks about how the orange juice they drink each day and the fruits they eat for dessert have many vitamins in them. Finally, she explains that the grains they eat provide lots of energy and that their favorite lean meats, chicken, and fish provide them with the protein they need. Esteban is glad to realize that his favorite dishes provide the nutrition his family needs!

When students have finished reading, ask them to answer the example question.

Example

Where does Esteban hear about the new food pyramid?

- (a.) In class
- b. In a restaurant
- c. On the playground
- d. In the kitchen

Once students have answered the example question, say:

*Did you circle the first answer, "In class"? That is the correct answer. Esteban hears about the new food pyramid in class. Now answer questions **five** through **nine**.*

5. What provides the family with the proteins they need?

- a. Vitamins and minerals
- b. Fruit juices
- (c.) Lean meats and fish
- d. Cakes and pies

6. What food has many vitamins in it?

   a. French fries
   b. Fruit
   c. Candy
   d. Tea

7. What does Esteban's dialogue with his mother help him to realize?

   a. That his favorite dishes are nutritious
   b. That his mother likes fruits
   c. That the food pyramid is not important
   d. That his mother is a good cook

C Allow students additional time to answer questions eight and nine.

8. Why is Esteban worried about his family's food choices?

   a. Because his family cannot eat a meal together
   b. Because he thinks his family is eating too many desserts
   c. Because he thinks his family is overeating
   d. Because he thinks his family's diet is not balanced

9. Why is Esteban's mother not worried about their diet?

   a. Because their diet includes all the food groups
   b. Because they only eat protein that is high in fat and cholesterol
   c. Because they eat beans and corn
   d. Because their diet is low in calories

A Read the following directions to the group:

Look at the example. It is the beginning of a sentence. You will write the rest of the sentence. You can write anything that makes sense to you, as long as it completes the sentence.

*Now do the **example**.*

> **Example**
>
> A balanced diet _____
> _____.

Observe students completing the example and assist them as necessary. Then, say:

Did you write something about a balanced diet? One answer could be "is important for good health." The sentence would be "A balanced diet is important for good health."

Be sure students understand the directions.

*Now finish the sentences for numbers **one** through **four**.*

1. The food pyramid _____
   _____.

2. We need protein to _____
   _____.

3. When you add fractions _____
   _____.

4. Photosynthesis _____
   _____.

B Read the following directions to the group:

You will use the blank lines to write three paragraphs. Each paragraph should be at least three sentences long. Remember to use capital letters and end punctuation.

*Now look at the **example**. There are three paragraphs, and each paragraph has information about coping with stress as part of a healthy lifestyle.*

The first paragraph explains why it's important to cope with stress, and says "Coping with stress or tension is hard to do. Yet it is important for healthy living. If you don't express your feelings, the situation will stay the same or become worse. This can make you feel sick."

The second paragraph presents suggestions about avoiding stress, and says "Do your best to prevent stressful events. If someone sits next to you in class and won't let you get your schoolwork done, change your seat. If the phone rings and you have an exam the next day, limit your conversation to five minutes and hang up. Stress prevention is all about making good choices."

The third paragraph is about coping with stress, and says "If you feel stressed, find someone that you can talk to about your problems. Caring for a pet or going for a long walk are also great ways to relax and feel better. Remember that reducing stress is an important part of a healthy lifestyle."

Example. Write three paragraphs about coping with stress as part of a healthy lifestyle.

> Coping with stress or tension is hard to do. Yet it is important for healthy living. If you don't express your feelings, the situation will stay the same or become worse. This can make you feel sick.
>
> Do your best to prevent stressful events. If someone sits next to you in class and won't let you get your schoolwork done, change your seat. If the phone rings and you have an exam the next day, limit the conversation to five minutes and hang up. Stress prevention is all about making good choices.
>
> If you feel stressed, find someone that you can talk to about your problems. Caring for a pet or going for a long walk are also great ways to relax and feel better. Remember that reducing stress is an important part of a healthy lifestyle.

*Now look at number **five**. Use the blank lines to write three paragraphs about how you can exercise to stay healthy.*

5. Write three paragraphs about how you can exercise to stay healthy.

Administer this assessment individually. Use the Speech Observation Form to record all responses.

A Direct the student's attention to the image on pages 112 and 113 in the Student Book. Use the picture to elicit a verbal response from the student. Say:

Look at this picture. I will ask you to talk about it.

1. *Point to and name three things in the picture.*

If the student responds in a language other than English, ask the student to respond in English (*Can you say it in English?*). If the student cannot name at least one item in the picture in English, stop and do not ask the rest of the questions.

B Ask the student to explain or describe something in the picture.

2. *What's this pyramid for?*

If the student gives a plausible but incorrect response, rephrase the question or ask the student for alternative responses. For instance, if the student says *It has food,* you may ask *What is the food pyramid used for?* If the student is unable to answer, stop and do not ask question 3.

C Ask the student to make inferences about the picture.

3. *Why is the food pyramid important?*

If the student gives a plausible but incomplete or incorrect response, rephrase the question or ask the student for alternative responses. For instance, if the student responds *It has food groups,* ask why we need to know the food groups.

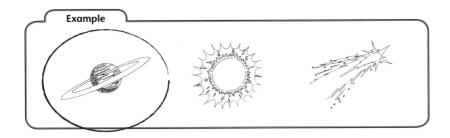

A Read the following directions to the group:

I'm going to ask you to draw a circle around one of the pictures.

*Let's do the **example**. Circle the picture of a planet.*

Example

Be sure students circle the correct answer.

*Look at number **one**. Circle the picture of a boulder.*

1.

*Look at number **two**. Circle the picture of a soldier.*

2.

*Look at number **three**. Circle the picture of a lightning bolt.*

3.

*Look at number **four**. Circle the picture of a pyramid.*

4.

B Read the following directions to the group:

I will read a story. Then, you will answer some questions about it by circling the correct picture. Now listen to the story.

> *In the war against the Titans, Zeus and his two brothers, Hades and Poseidon, fought many battles with all their might. Zeus threw his lightening bolts at the Titans. Strong winds roared and pulled up many trees from the earth. Then, Gaia, Zeus's mother, came up with a plan because she wanted her sons to win. Zeus followed his mother's plan. Finally, the war against the Titans was over. The three brothers had won. After the battle, Zeus divided the world with his siblings. Zeus became king of the gods and ruler of the sky, Hades ruled the underworld, and Poseidon ruled the sea.*

Let's do the **example**. *What did Zeus become after the battle with the Titans? Circle the picture.*

Observe students completing the example and assist them as necessary. Then, say:

Zeus became king of the gods after the battle with the Titans. Did you circle the picture of the king? That is the answer.

Let's do number **five**. *What did Zeus throw at the Titans? Circle the picture.*

5.

Let's do number **six**. *What did the strong winds pull up from the earth?*

6.

Let's do number **seven**. *What did Zeus give Poseidon to rule over?*

7.

C Read the following directions to the group:

Now I'm going to ask you some more questions about the story. For each question, I'll read four answers. Circle the letter of the correct answer.

Let's do the example. In the story, what did Zeus give Hades to rule?

*If it was the **sea**, circle the letter **a**.*

*If it was the **underworld**, circle the letter **b**.*

*If it was the **earth**, circle the letter **c**.*

*If it was the **sky**, circle the letter **d**.*

Observe students completing the example and assist them as necessary. Then, say:

In the story, Zeus gave Hades the underworld to rule. Did you circle the letter b? *That is the answer.*

*Let's do number **eight**. Who fought against Zeus, Hades, and Poseidon?*

*If it was the **Titans**, circle the letter **a**.*

*If it was the **Olympians**, circle the letter **b**.*

*If it was **Gaia**, circle the letter **c**.*

*If it was the **Romans**, circle the letter **d**.*

*Let's do number **nine**. Why did Gaia help Zeus?*

*If it was because she **wanted to be queen**, circle the letter **a**.*

*If it was because she **liked Zeus best**, circle the letter **b**.*

*If it was because she **felt sorry for Zeus**, circle the letter **c**.*

*If it was because she **wanted her sons to win the war**, circle the letter **d**.*

A Read the following directions to the group:

Look at the sentences. A word is missing from each one. Circle the word that completes the sentence.

Now do the **example**.

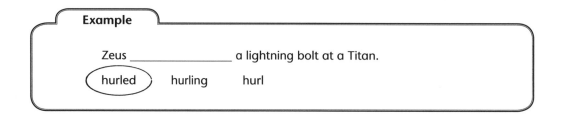

> **Example**
>
> Zeus _____ a lightning bolt at a Titan.
>
> (hurled)   hurling   hurl

Observe students completing the example and assist them as necessary. Then, say:

Did you circle the first word, hurled? *That is the correct word. Zeus* hurled *a lightning bolt at a Titan.*

Be sure students circle the correct answer.

Now circle the words for numbers **one** *through* **four**.

1.   Zeus _____ to Gaia's advice.

gave   (listened)   snatched

2.   Metis ruled with _____ and knowledge.

(wisdom)   throne   vain

3.   The goddess of _____ taught humans how to grow food.

eat   tradition   (agriculture)

4.   Our solar system is part of a _____ known as the Milky Way.

planet   (galaxy)   satellite

B Read the following directions to the group:

Read the story. Then, you will answer some questions about it. For each question, circle the correct answer.

> In the beginning, darkness was everywhere. In the darkness, there was only an egg. Pangu slept and grew inside the egg. Pangu grew to a gigantic size. Finally, he stretched his enormous arms and legs, cracking the egg open. Part of the egg floated up to form the sky, and part of the egg sank to become the earth. To make sure that the earth and the sky stayed separate, he placed his head in the sky and his feet on the earth. As time passed, he grew and grew, pushing the sky and the earth farther apart. His breath made the wind and the clouds. His voice made thunder and lightning. His eyes became the sun and the moon. Pangu was pleased with his creation because of the beauty of the earth and the sky.

When students have finished reading, ask them to answer the example question.

Example

What is the story about?

(a.) The creation of the sky and the earth

b. Pangu's eyes

c. The darkness of the night

d. The cracking of an egg

Once students have answered the example question, say:

*Did you circle the first answer, "The creation of the sky and the earth"? That is the correct answer. The story is about the creation of the sky and the earth. Now answer questions **five** through **nine**.*

5.   Where did Pangu sleep and grow?

   a.   Inside his house

   b.   In his bedroom

   (c.) Inside an egg

   d.   Under his blankets

6. What did his eyes turn into?

   (a.) The sun and the moon
   b. The sky and the earth
   c. The wind and the rain
   d. The stars and comets

7. What did his breath turn into?

   a. Rivers and lakes
   (b.) Wind and clouds
   c. Hurricanes and tornadoes
   d. Fog and mist

C Allow students additional time to answer questions eight and nine.

8. Why was Pangu pleased?

   a. Because his food tasted good
   (b.) Because his creation was beautiful
   c. Because his work was done
   d. Because his party was fun

9. How did the egg crack?

   a. It cracked when Pangu dropped it.
   b. It cracked when Pangu cut it.
   c. It cracked when Pangu hammered it.
   (d.) It cracked when Pangu stretched his enormous arms and legs.

A Read the following directions to the group:

Look at the example. It is the beginning of a sentence. You will write the rest of the sentence. You can write anything that makes sense to you, as long as it completes the sentence.

*Now do the **example**.*

> **Example**
>
> The sun _____
> _____ .

Observe students completing the example and assist them as necessary. Then, say:

Did you write something about the sun? One answer could be "is a star at the center of our solar system." The sentence would be "The sun is a star at the center of our solar system."

Be sure students understand the directions.

*Now finish the sentences for numbers **one** through **four**.*

1. The Titans were _____
   _____ .

2. A myth is _____
   _____ .

3. Vikings' navigation depended _____
   _____ .

4. The outer planets _____
   _____ .

B Read the following directions to the group:

You will use the blank lines to write three paragraphs. Each paragraph should be at least three sentences long. Remember to use capital letters and end punctuation.

*Now look at the **example**. There are three paragraphs about an Olympian god.*

The first paragraph is about who the god is, and says "Zeus became the king of the gods. He lived on Mount Olympus. He was the youngest son of Gaia and Cronos."

The second paragraph is about what the god did, and says "He fought a great war against the Titans. He freed the three Cyclopes and the three Hecatonchires from prison. With the help of the Cyclopes and the Hecatonchires, Zeus defeated the Titans and put them in prison."

The third paragraph is about why the god is important, and says "Zeus fought many battles. He was a very powerful king. He is remembered for his courage and his leadership."

Example. Write three paragraphs about an Olympian god.

> Zeus became the king of the gods. He lived on Mount Olympus. He was the youngest son of Gaia and Cronos.
>
> He fought a great war against the Titans. He freed the three Cyclopes and the three Hecatonchires from prison. With the help of the Cyclopes and the Hecatonchires, Zeus defeated the Titans and put them in prison.
>
> Zeus fought many battles. He was a very powerful king. He is remembered for his courage and his leadership.

*Now look at number **five**. Use the blank lines to write three paragraphs about your favorite superhero from mythology, from a book, or from TV.*

5. Write three paragraphs about your favorite superhero from mythology, from a book, or from TV.

Administer this assessment individually. Use the Speech Observation Form to record all responses.

A Direct the student's attention to the image on pages 146 and 147 in the Student Book. Use the picture to elicit a verbal response from the student. Say:

Look at this picture. I will ask you to talk about it.

1. *Point to and name three things in the picture.*

If the student responds in a language other than English, ask the student to respond in English (*Can you say it in English?*). If the student cannot name at least one item in the picture in English, stop and do not ask the rest of the questions.

B Ask the student to explain or describe something in the picture.

2. *What's the older man doing?*

If the student gives a plausible but incorrect response, rephrase the question or ask the student for alternative responses. For instance, if the student says *Talking*, you may ask *What do you think he is talking about?* If the student is unable to answer, stop and do not ask question 3.

C Ask the student to make inferences about the picture.

3. *Why is the group of people listening to the older man?*

If the student gives a plausible but incomplete or incorrect response, rephrase the question or ask the student for alternative responses. For instance, if the student responds *They like to*, ask *Why do you think they like to listen to the old man?*

A Read the following directions to the group:

I'm going to ask you to draw a circle around one of the pictures.

*Let's do the **example**. Circle the picture of a kite.*

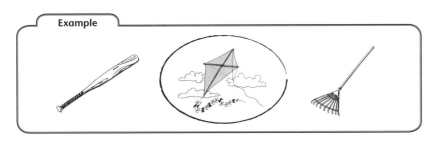

Be sure students circle the correct answer.

*Look at number **one**. Circle the picture of bifocals.*

1.

*Look at number **two**. Circle the picture of static electricity.*

2.

*Look at number **three**. Circle the picture of Benjamin Franklin conducting an experiment.*

3.

*Look at number **four**. Circle the picture of a historical figure in the United States.*

4.

67

B Read the following directions to the group:

I will read a story. Then, you will answer some questions about it by circling the correct picture. Now listen to the story.

> One stormy afternoon, Joshua looked out of his window. He saw his neighbor, Benjamin Franklin, flying a kite! Joshua knew Benjamin Franklin was always doing something interesting. He knew that Franklin's ideas helped his own family. Franklin had convinced Joshua's father to get all of his children vaccinated against smallpox. Also, Joshua's father wore glasses, called "double spectacles," which Franklin had invented. Now, his father could see close for reading and also at a distance. When Joshua went outside, Franklin told him that he was doing an experiment with a kite and a key because he wanted to find out if lightning was a form of electricity.

Let's do the **example**. *What was the weather like on the afternoon that Joshua saw Benjamin Franklin flying a kite? Circle the picture.*

Example

Observe students completing the example and assist them as necessary. Then, say:
The weather was stormy. Did you circle the picture of a rainstorm? That is the answer.

Let's do number **five**. *What was Benjamin Franklin doing outside that afternoon?*

5.

Let's do number **six**. *What invention helped Joshua's father to see better?*

6.

Let's do number **seven**. *What did Benjamin Franklin want Joshua's family to do to prevent smallpox?*

7.

c Read the following directions to the group:

Now I'm going to ask you some more questions about the story. For each question, I'll read four answers. Circle the letter of the correct answer.

*Let's do the **example**. What invention of Benjamin Franklin's helped Joshua's father to see close for reading and at a distance?*

*If it was **double spectacles**, circle the letter **a**.*

*If it was a **magnifying glass**, circle the letter **b**.*

*If it was a **vaccine**, circle the letter **c**.*

*If it was a **book with large print**, circle the letter **d**.*

Observe students completing the example and assist them as necessary. Then, say:

Double spectacles was the invention of Benjamin Franklin that helped Joshua's father see close for reading and at a distance. Did you circle the letter a*? That is the answer.*

*Let's do number **eight**. Why did Joshua go outside to find out what Benjamin Franklin was doing?*

*If it is because **it was dark and stormy**, circle the letter **a**.*

*If it is because **Benjamin Franklin was always doing something interesting**, circle the letter **b**.*

*If it is because **Joshua liked to fly kites**, circle the letter **c**.*

*If it is because **Benjamin Franklin was giving inoculations**, circle the letter **d**.*

*Let's do number **nine**. Why was Benjamin Franklin experimenting with a kite and a key in the rain?*

*If it was because he wanted **people to see what he was doing**, circle the letter **a**.*

*If it was because he wanted **to hear the thunder**, circle the letter **b**.*

*If it was because he wanted **to try out a new kite**, circle the letter **c**.*

*If it was because he wanted **to find out if lightning was a form of electricity**, circle the letter **d**.*

A Read the following directions to the group:

Look at the sentences. A word is missing from each one. Circle the word that completes the sentence.

Now do the **example**.

Example

The word "trees" _____ with the word "seas."

stanzas   similes   (rhymes)

Observe students completing the example and assist them as necessary. Then, say:

Did you circle the third word, rhymes? *The word "trees" rhymes with the word "seas."*

Be sure students circle the correct answer.

Now circle the words for numbers **one** *through* **four**.

---

1. Franklin was successful in his business because he was
   a _____ worker.
   (diligent)   suspicious   eloquent

---

2. Noah Webster's _____ to education were as celebrated
   as Franklin's inventions.
   (contributions)   controversial   boycott

---

3. "She was a fish in the water" is an example of a _____.
   rhyme   simile   (metaphor)

---

4. The average age of the students is called the _____.
   median   (mean)   mode

B Read the following directions to the group:

Read the story. Then, you will answer some questions about it. For each question, circle the correct answer.

> Lisa's class was studying the contributions of the country's founders. Lisa decided she wanted to know more about the Declaration of Independence. She learned that it was written during the Second Continental Congress in 1776. Thomas Jefferson was the main author because he was an eloquent writer. He could clearly state the sentiments and thoughts of the men of the Congress. Jefferson did have help from a committee. Benjamin Franklin, John Adams, Roger Sherman, and Robert R. Livingston helped him list the rights of self-government, life, liberty, and the pursuit of happiness. Lisa was glad that she lived in the United States because of these inalienable rights in the Declaration of Independence.

When students have finished reading, ask them to answer the example question.

Example

Who was the main author of the Declaration of Independence?

(a.) Thomas Jefferson

b. George Washington

c. Noah Webster

d. King George

Once students have answered the example question, say:

*Did you circle the first answer, "Thomas Jefferson"? That is the correct answer. Thomas Jefferson was the main author of the Declaration of Independence. Now answer questions **five** through **nine**.*

5. What document did Lisa want to know more about?

    a. The Pledge of Allegiance

    b. The Constitution of the United States

    (c.) The Declaration of Independence

    d. The American English dictionary

6. What was Lisa's class studying?

    (a.) The contributions of the country's founders

    b. The contributions of England to the United States

    c. The pamphlets of the Continental Congress

    d. The challenges of writing important documents

7. When was the Declaration of Independence written?

    a. During the committee's trip to England

    (b.) During the Continental Congress in 1776

    c. During the school year in 2006

    d. During the pursuit of happiness

C Allow students additional time to answer questions eight and nine.

8. Why was Thomas Jefferson the main author of the Declaration of Independence?

    a. Because he was the president of the country

    b. Because his friends liked him

    c. Because he knew the laws of the nation

    (d.) Because he was a very good writer

9. Why was Lisa glad that she lived in the United States?

    (a.) Because of the inalienable rights in the Declaration of Independence

    b. Because she could do whatever she wanted

    c. Because of the amount of money you can make

    d. Because of the good schools in the country

A Read the following directions to the group:

Look at the example. It is the beginning of a sentence. You will write the rest of the sentence. You can write anything that makes sense to you, as long as it completes the sentence.

*Now do the **example**.*

> **Example**
>
> Benjamin Franklin _____
>
> _____.

Observe students completing the example and assist them as necessary. Then, say:

Did you write something about Benjamin Franklin? One answer could be "was an American inventor." The sentence would be "Benjamin Franklin was an American inventor."

Be sure students understand the directions.

*Now finish the sentences for numbers **one** through **four**.*

1. An apprentice _____

   _____.

2. The boycott _____

   _____.

3. Static electricity _____

   _____.

4. A metaphor _____

   _____.

B Read the following directions to the group:

You will use the blank lines to write three paragraphs. Each paragraph should be at least three sentences long. Remember to use capital letters and end punctuation.

Now look at the **example**. *There are three paragraphs about John Hancock, one of the founders of the United States of America.*

The first paragraph is about who John Hancock is, and says "John Hancock was a well-known and very popular historical figure in the United States of America. He played an instrumental role in the American Revolution and was the first to sign the Declaration of Independence. Hancock's signature on the Declaration is the most easily recognizable of all."

The second paragraph is about his life, and says "John Hancock was born in Braintree, Massachusetts, in 1737. He attended Harvard College for a business education. Soon his intelligence and wealth made him a very powerful man.

The third paragraph is about why he is important, and says "John Hancock joined with other prominent leaders to promote independence from Great Britain. His dignity and character inspired many people to fight for their right to self-government. John Hancock will never be forgotten for his contribution to the founding of this country."

Example. Write three paragraphs about John Hancock, one of the founders of the United States of America.

> John Hancock was a well-known and very popular historical figure in the United States of America. He played an instrumental role in the American Revolution and was the first to sign the Declaration of Independence. Hancock's signature on the Declaration is the most easily recognizable of all.
>
> John Hancock was born in Braintree, Massachusetts, in 1737. He attended Harvard College for a business education. Soon his intelligence and wealth made him a very powerful man.
>
> Hancock joined with other prominent leaders to promote independence from Great Britain. His dignity and character inspired many people to fight for their right to self-government. John Hancock will never be forgotten for his contribution to the founding of this country.

Now look at number **five**. *Use the blank lines to write three paragraphs about one of the founders of the United States of America.*

5. Write three paragraphs about one of the founders of the United States of America.

Administer this assessment individually. Use the Speech Observation Form to record all responses.

A Direct the student's attention to the image on page 181 in the Student Book. Use the picture to elicit a verbal response from the student. Say:

Look at this picture. I will ask you to talk about it.

1. *Point to and name three things in the picture.*

If the student responds in a language other than English, ask the student to respond in English (*Can you say it in English?*). If the student cannot name at least one item in the picture in English, stop and do not ask the rest of the questions.

B Ask the student to explain or describe something in the picture.

2. *What's the man doing?*

If the student gives a plausible but incorrect response, rephrase the question or ask the student for alternative responses. For instance, if the student says *He standing,* you may ask *What's he doing standing there?* If the student is unable to answer, stop and do not ask question 3.

C Ask the student to make inferences about the picture.

3. *Why is the boy pointing to the key?*

If the student gives a plausible but incomplete or incorrect response, rephrase the question or ask the student for alternative responses. For instance, if the student responds *He pointing,* ask why the boy is pointing.

A Read the following directions to the group:

I'm going to ask you to draw a circle around one of the pictures.

*Let's do the **example**. Circle the picture of leaves.*

Be sure students circle the correct answer.

*Look at number **one**. Circle the picture of a biome that is hot and arid.*

1.

*Look at number **two**. Circle the picture of an animal that hibernates.*

2.

*Look at number **three**. Circle the picture of people logging.*

3.

*Look at number **four**. Circle the picture of a conifer, or evergreen tree.*

4.

B Read the following directions to the group:

I will read a story. Then, you will answer some questions about it by circling the correct picture. Now listen to the story.

> *We produce waste in many of our daily activities. Much of our waste is a threat that endangers the delicate ecosystems of the earth's biomes. Food products are biodegradable waste. This is good because "biodegradable" means that the waste can break down over time to decompose into soil. Some waste cannot be broken down and decompose. That is why recycling is so important. "Recycling" means making new products from waste. Recycling is done when you separate recyclable materials from other trash. Have you ever seen the triangular loop of arrows on a soda or juice can? That symbol lets you know that the item can be recycled. When we recycle, we reduce the amount of material in landfills. We need to recycle because it will keep ecosystems from being disrupted.*

*Let's do the **example**. What do we produce in many of our daily activities? Circle the picture.*

Example

Observe students completing the example and assist them as necessary. Then, say:
We produce waste. Did you circle the picture of waste? That is the answer.
*Let's do number **five**. Which product is biodegradable? Circle the picture.*

5.

*Let's do number **six**. What can we do to reduce the amount of material in landfills?*

6.

*Let's do number **seven**. Which product should you recycle? Circle the picture.*

7.

C Read the following directions to the group:

Now I'm going to ask you some more questions about the story. For each question, I'll read four answers. Circle the letter of the correct answer.

*Let's do the **example**. Where does waste go if we do not recycle?*

*If it goes to a **landfill**, circle the letter **a**.*

*If it goes to a **recycling bin**, circle the letter **b**.*

*If it goes to a **refrigerator**, circle the letter **c**.*

*If it goes to a **stove**, circle the letter **d**.*

Observe students completing the example and assist them as necessary. Then, say:

Waste goes to landfills if we do not recycle. Did you circle the letter a? That is the answer.

*Let's do number **eight**. Why do some items have a triangular loop of arrows on them?*

*If it's because **the item will look nicer**, circle the letter **a**.*

*If it's because **it needs to be sent to a landfill**, circle the letter **b**.*

*If it's because **the item is recyclable**, circle the letter **c**.*

*If it's because **people should keep the item**, circle the letter **d**.*

*Let's do number **nine**. Why do we need to recycle?*

*If it's because **recycling helps you stay healthy**, circle the letter **a**.*

*If it's because **recycling helps the trash to smell good**, circle the letter **b**.*

*If it's because **food tastes better if it is recycled**, circle the letter **c**.*

*If it's because **recycling helps keep ecosystems from being disrupted**, circle the letter **d**.*

A Read the following directions to the group:

Look at the sentences. A word is missing from each one. Circle the word that completes the sentence.

*Now do the **example**.*

> **Example**
>
> Forests are the _____ diverse ecological system.
>
> ⟨ most ⟩   more   equal

Observe students completing the example and assist them as necessary. Then, say:

Did you circle the first word, most? *That is the correct word. Forests are the* most *diverse ecological system.*

Be sure students circle the correct answer.

*Now circle the words for numbers **one** through **four**.*

1. Deforestation can cause global _____.

   precipitation   ⟨ warming ⟩   hibernation

2. Desert animals that come out at night are called _____.

   ⟨ nocturnal ⟩   migratory   arid

3. A _____ biome is covered with grass and has few trees.

   tundra   desert   ⟨ grassland ⟩

4. Tropical grasslands called _____ are found in Australia and East Africa.

   aquifers   ⟨ savannas ⟩   taigas

B Read the following directions to the group:

Read the story. Then, you will answer some questions about it. For each question, circle the correct answer.

> Daniel's family lived in a forest. They harvested the evergreen trees that grew near his home, but Daniel was concerned about the ecological consequences of logging. He decided to write a report on deforestation and its threat to the once-abundant trees. He told his family about his report. His father got angry because he thought Daniel did not like the kind of work that he did. Then, Daniel showed him the scientific evidence about deforestation and climate change. His father agreed that it was a serious problem. The next day, they talked about the impact of logging on the forest biome. Together they read books and articles to see what to do about the problem. They decided they would work toward increasing biodiversity and reducing global warming by planting many types of trees and flowering plants. Daniel was glad that they were doing something to protect the endangered ecosystems.

When students have finished reading, ask them to answer the example question.

> **Example**
>
> Where did Daniel live?
>
> (a.) In a forest
> b.   In a desert
> c.   In a large city
> d.   In a log cabin

Once students have answered the example question, say:

*Did you circle the first answer, "In a forest"? That is the correct answer. Daniel lived in a forest. Now answer questions **five** through **nine**.*

5. What did Daniel's family harvest?

   (a.) Evergreen trees
   b.   Deciduous trees
   c.   Vegetables
   d.   Fruits

6. What did Daniel write a report about?

    a. Protection of the rain forest

    b. Endangered ecosystems

    (c.) Deforestation and its threat to the trees

    d. Gardening for vegetables to eat

7. What did Daniel and his father do together?

    (a.) Read books and articles about deforestation

    b. Played soccer in the forest

    c. Cut down all the trees around their home

    d. Read books and articles about growing a vegetable garden

C Allow students additional time to answer questions eight and nine.

8. What did his father do when Daniel showed him scientific evidence about deforestation and climate change?

    a. He didn't believe Daniel.

    b. He taught Daniel how to harvest trees.

    c. He said that logging didn't harm the ecosystem.

    (d.) He agreed that deforestation was a serious problem.

9. Why did Daniel and his father decide to plant many types of trees and flowering plants?

    (a.) Because it would help protect the environment

    b. Because it would make their forest look more interesting

    c. Because they could make more money

    d. Because they wanted to do a father-and-son project

A Read the following directions to the group:

Look at the example. It is the beginning of a sentence. You will write the rest of the sentence. You can write anything that makes sense to you, as long as it completes the sentence.

*Now do the **example**.*

> **Example**
>
> Ecosystems are _____
> _____ .

Observe students completing the example and assist them as necessary. Then, say:

Did you write what ecosystems are? One answer could be "groups of plants and animals that need each other for survival." The sentence would be "Ecosystems are groups of plants and animals that need each other for survival."

Be sure students understand the directions.

*Now finish the sentences for numbers **one** through **four**.*

1. An aquifer _____
    _____ .

2. Global warming _____
    _____ .

3. Science fiction _____
    _____ .

4. The tundra _____
    _____ .

B Read the following directions to the group:

Use the blank lines to write three paragraphs. Each paragraph should be at least three sentences long. Remember to use capital letters and end punctuation.

*Now look at the **example**. There are three paragraphs that tell a fictional story about the future on planet Earth.*

The first paragraph describes the setting and the characters, and says "My name is Rosa. Rosa means *rose* in English. It is the name of a flower that used to grow before the earth's surface turned to ice. My grandparents tell us stories about how the earth was warm and green when they were children."

The second paragraph tells about important events and new technology, and says "My family lives in a microcommunity, which is is like a self-contained biome. Here we grow plants for food. If we went outside our microcommunity, we would not survive the cold."

The third paragraph makes a statement about the effects of climate change, and says "Our planet is a cold and barren place except in the communities where people live. My grandparents tell me about the many beautiful flowers that used to grow here. I wish that people had taken care of the earth back then. If they had, my name would be more than just a name to me."

Example. Write three paragraphs that tell a fictional story about the future on planet Earth.

> My name is Rosa. Rosa means *rose* in English. It is the name of a flower that used to grow before the earth's surface turned to ice. My grandparents tell us stories about how the earth was warm and green when they were children.
>
> My family lives in a microcommunity, which is like a self-contained biome. Here we grow plants for food. If we went outside our microcommunity, we would not survive the cold.
>
> Our planet is a cold and barren place except in the communities where people live. My grandparents tell me about the many beautiful flowers that used to grow here. I wish that people had taken care of the earth back then. If they had, my name would be more than just a name to me.

*Now look at number **five**. Use the blank lines to write three paragraphs that tell a fictional story about what life on Earth will be like in the future if the climate keeps changing.*

5. Write three paragraphs that tell a fiction story about what life on Earth will be like in the future if the climate keeps changing.

Administer this assessment individually. Use the Speech Observation Form to record all responses.

A Direct the student's attention to the image on pages 244 in the Student Book. Use the picture to elicit a verbal response from the student. Say:

Look at this picture. I will ask you to talk about it.

1. *Point to and name three things in the picture.*

If the student responds in a language other than English, ask the student to respond in English (*Can you say it in English?*). If the student cannot name at least one item in the picture in English, stop and do not ask the rest of the questions.

B Ask the student to explain or describe something in the picture.

2. *What's the boy doing?*

If the student gives a plausible but incorrect response, rephrase the question or ask the student for alternative responses. For instance, if the student says *He's taking trash out,* you may ask *What kind of trash is he taking out?* If the student is unable to answer, stop and do not ask question 3.

C Ask the student to make inferences about the picture.

3. *Why is the boy recycling the trash?*

If the student gives a plausible but incomplete or incorrect response, rephrase the question or ask the student for alternative responses. For instance, if the student responds *He's recycling,* ask why he or she thinks the boy is recycling.

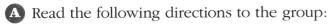

A Read the following directions to the group:

I'm going to ask you to draw a circle around one of the pictures.

*Let's do the **example**. Circle the picture of a map.*

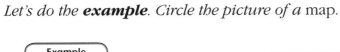

Be sure students circle the correct answer.

*Look at number **one**. Circle the picture of a* telescope.

*Look at number **two**. Circle the picture of a* space probe.

*Look at number **three**. Circle the picture of a* compass rose.

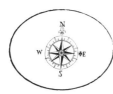

*Look at number **four**. Circle the picture of* livestock.

B Read the following directions to the group:

I will read a story. Then, you will answer some questions about it by circling the correct picture. Now listen to the story.

> *May 12*
>
>   *I like to write in this journal that my friends gave me before we left town. It even has my name painted on it: Luis. Today is the first day of our expedition to find a land route from Baja to Alta California. My job is to be an assistant to the cartographer. The cartographer must draw accurate maps of the route. Today we traveled in a wilderness of shrubs and trees. When we made camp at the end of the day, we were all hungry and tired. We were glad we had brought livestock with us because we could have something to eat. We had a scare, though, when a group of Native Americans entered our camp. I'm glad they were friendly. This has been a long and exciting day. I wonder what tomorrow will bring?*

*Let's do the **example**. What does Luis like to do? Circle the picture.*

Observe students completing the example and assist them as necessary. Then, say:

Luis likes to write. Did you circle the picture of Luis writing? That is the answer.

*Let's do number **five**. What does a cartographer draw? Circle the picture.*

5.

*Let's do number **six**. Where did the expedition begin?*

6.

*Let's do number **seven**. What type of land did the expedition travel through the first day?*

7.

C Read the following directions to the group:

Now I'm going to ask you some more questions about the story. For each question, I'll read four answers. Circle the letter of the correct answer.

*Let's do the **example**. Why did the expedition have a scare the first night?*

*If it was because **a group of Native Americans entered the camp**, circle the letter **a**.*

*If it was because **a strange animal entered the camp**, circle the letter **b**.*

*If it was because **the camp caught on fire**, circle the letter **c**.*

*If it was because **the cartographer quit**, circle the letter **d**.*

Observe students completing the example and assist them as necessary. Then, say:

The expedition had a scare the first night because a group of Native Americans entered the camp. Did you circle the letter a? That is the answer.

*Let's do number **eight**. Why were the explorers glad that they had brought livestock with them?*

*If it was because **they would have food to eat on the expedition**, circle the letter **a**.*

*If it was because **they liked taking care of the livestock**, circle the letter **b**.*

*If it was because **the livestock protected them from the Natives** circle the letter **c**.*

*If it was because **the livestock made it easier to travel**, circle the letter **d**.*

*Let's do number **nine**. Why did the expedition make this journey?*

*If it was to **find gold and silver**, circle the letter **a**.*

*If it was to **write in their journals**, circle the letter **b**.*

*If it was to **go live with the Native Americans**, circle the letter **c**.*

*If it was to **find a land route to Alta California**, circle the letter **d**.*

A Read the following directions to the group:

Look at the sentences. A word is missing from each one. Circle the word that completes the sentence.

*Now do the **example**.*

> **Example**
>
> A _____ includes a scale, a compass rose, and a legend.
>
> cartographer (map) chronometer

Observe students completing the example and assist them as necessary. Then, say:

Did you circle the second word, map*? That is the correct word. A* map *includes a scale, a compass rose, and a legend.*

Be sure students circle the correct answer.

*Now circle the words for numbers **one** through **four**.*

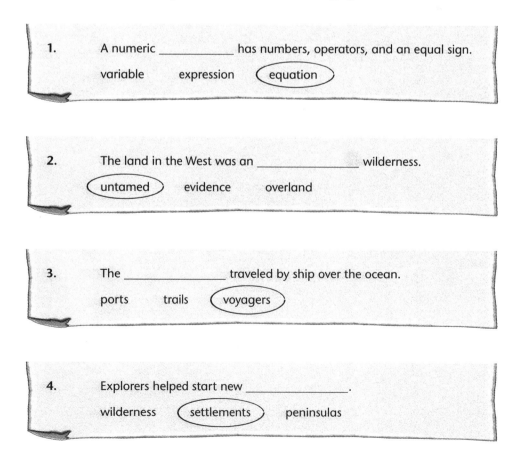

1. A numeric _____ has numbers, operators, and an equal sign.

variable   expression   (equation)

2. The land in the West was an _____ wilderness.

(untamed)   evidence   overland

3. The _____ traveled by ship over the ocean.

ports   trails   (voyagers)

4. Explorers helped start new _____.

wilderness   (settlements)   peninsulas

B Read the following directions to the group:

Read the story. Then, you will answer some questions about it. For each question, circle the correct answer.

> Lupe heard her parents talk about a family ancestor. She thought that her ancestor had lived a very interesting life, so she decided to find out more about him. Lupe had heard that this ancestor was part of the expedition that found a route from Baja to Alta California. Her family had old letters and a journal that she could use to learn more about his expedition. The journal was about his journey through the wilderness. Some entries in the journal described times when the explorers were lost and how Native Americans served as guides. Native American guides were seasoned hunters and trappers. They led the expedition to established trails. The explorer's claim that they were making discoveries in a new world was not exactly true, and they knew it. It only meant that it was a new world to people like them, who had come from so far away.

When students have finished reading, ask them to answer the example question.

Example

What did Lupe decide to do?

a. Find out about her ancestor
b. Explore stories of Native Americans
c. Go on an expedition
d. Write a journal about her parents

Once students have answered the example question, say:

*Did you circle the first answer, "Find out about her ancestor"? That is the correct answer. Lupe decided to find out about her ancestor. Now answer questions **five** through **nine**.*

5.   What did the journal recount?

    a.   The Native American dances
    b.   The maps of Alta California
    c.   The journey through the wilderness
    d.   The animals and plants of Baja California

6. What were some of the journal entries about?

- (a.) When the explorers were lost
- b. When the explorers went hunting
- c. When the explorers got sick
- d. When the explorers finally made it home again

7. Where did the Native American guides lead the explorers?

- a. To their village
- (b.) To established trails
- c. To the traps
- d. To a settlement

C Allow students additional time to answer questions eight and nine.

8. Why did Lupe decide to explore her family story?

- a. Because she wanted to learn how to write in a journal
- b. Because she wanted to be a historian
- c. Because she was studying explorers in school
- (d.) Because she wanted to learn about her ancestor

9. Why did the explorers think their discoveries were new only to those who had come from so far away?

- (a.) Because many people were already living there
- b. Because the plants and animals were the same
- c. Because the journey had been long and hard
- d. Because many people said the same thing

A Read the following directions to the group:

Look at the example. It is the beginning of a sentence. You will write the rest of the sentence. You can write anything that makes sense to you, as long as it completes the sentence.

*Now do the **example**.*

> **Example**
>
> Early explorers _____
> _____.

Observe students completing the example and assist them as necessary. Then, say:

Did you write something that early explorers did? One answer could be "helped find new land routes." The sentence would be "Early explorers helped find new land routes."

Be sure students understand the directions.

*Now finish the sentences for numbers **one** through **four**.*

1. The untamed wilderness _____
   _____.

2. A map _____
   _____.

3. An algebraic equation _____
   _____.

4. A molecule _____
   _____.

B Read the following directions to the group:

You will use the blank lines to write three paragraphs. Each paragraph should be at least three sentences long. Remember to use capital letters and end punctuation.

*Now look at the **example**. There are three paragraphs that make up a journal entry about a trip.*

The first paragraph describes the event, and says "Today I came to visit my grandmother. She lives on the East Coast, and I live on the West Coast. It was a long way to travel. I traveled alone on an airplane for the first time."

The second paragraph discusses the challenges faced during the trip, and says "At the airport, my parents could not go past the security gate. I had to leave them behind. Everyone was in a hurry to get through security, but I didn't know what to do. At that moment, someone from the airline came up to ask if I needed help. She took me to the departure gate. We got on the plane and started talking."

The third paragraph describes thoughts and feelings, and says "Traveling alone for the first time was a scary experience. I was worried I wouldn't land in the right city. I was afraid I would miss my plane. None of those things happened. I arrived safely, and my grandmother was right here to greet me. Today I learned not to be afraid to ask for help."

Example. Write a three-paragraph journal entry about a trip.

> Today I came to visit my grandmother. She lives on the East Coast, and I live on the West Coast. It was a long way to travel. I traveled alone on an airplane for the first time.
>
> At the airport, my parents could not go past the security gate. I had to leave them behind. Everyone was in a hurry to get through security, but I didn't know what to do. At that moment, someone from the airline came up to ask if I needed help. She took me to the departure gate. We got on the plane and started talking.
>
> Traveling alone for the first time was a scary experience. I was worried I wouldn't land in the right city. I was afraid I would miss my plane. None of those things happened. I arrived safely, and my grandmother was right here to greet me. Today I learned not to be afraid to ask for help.

*Now look at number **five**. Use the blank lines to write a three-paragraph journal entry about a new experience or a memorable event in a place you visited for the first time.*

5. Write a three-paragraph journal entry about a new experience or a memorable event in a place you visited for the first time.

Administer this assessment individually. Use the Speech Observation Form to record all responses.

A Direct the student's attention to the image on page 248 in the Student Book. Use the picture to elicit a verbal response from the student. Say:

Look at this picture. I will ask you to talk about it.

1. *Point to and name three things in the picture.*

If the student responds in a language other than English, ask the student to respond in English (*Can you say it in English?*). If the student cannot name at least one item in the picture in English, stop and do not ask the rest of the questions.

B Ask the student to explain or describe something in the picture.

2. *What are the people doing?*

If the student gives a plausible but incorrect response, rephrase the question or ask the student for alternative responses. For instance, if the student says *They are going,* you may ask *Where do you think they are going?* If the student is unable to answer, stop and do not ask question 3.

C Ask the student to make inferences about the picture.

3. *Why are the people taking animals and supplies?*

If the student gives a plausible but incomplete or incorrect response, rephrase the question or ask the student for alternative responses. For instance, if the student responds *They're going on a trip,* ask why they need supplies for the trip.

Post-Assessment

A Read the following directions to the group:

I'm going to ask you to draw a circle around one of the pictures.

*Let's do the **example**. Circle the picture of a* fruit.

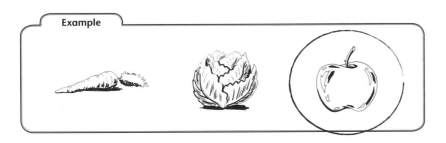

Be sure students circle the correct answer.
*Look at number **one**. Circle the picture of a* fish.

1.

*Look at number **two**. Circle the picture of* eyes.

2.
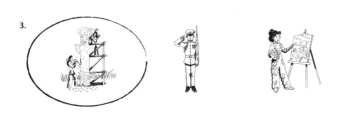

*Look at number **three**. Circle the picture of a* sculptor.

3.

*Look at number **four**. Circle the picture of a* helmet.

4.

*Look at number **five**. Circle the picture of a* battle.

5.

*Look at number **six**. Circle the picture of* someone writing in a journal.

6.

*Look at number **seven**. Circle the picture of a* grocery store.

7.

B Read the following directions to the group:

I will read a story. Then, you will answer some questions about it by circling the correct picture. Now listen to the story.

> *Many years ago, people began studying the movements of the stars and the planets. They learned that in our solar system, eight planets orbit the sun. They even learned that the solar system is part of a galaxy called the Milky Way. But still, no one had been beyond the earth's atmosphere. In the 1960s, people learned how to fly outside of the earth's atmosphere into outer space. They built spacecraft to take people there. The people who fly the spacecraft are called astronauts. Using the spacecraft, astronauts could fly to the moon. There is no oxygen in outer space, so astronauts have to take along special gear that allows them to go outside the spacecraft. This gear allows them to breathe and keeps them from freezing. Many discoveries and technological advances had to happen before spacecrafts could fly into outer space, and flying into space is still very dangerous today. One day, people may fly to another planet!*

Let's do the **example**. *Who goes into outer space? Circle the picture.*

Observe students completing the example and assist them as necessary. Then, say:

Astronauts go into outer space. Did you circle the picture of the astronaut? That is the answer.

Let's do number **eight**. *How do astronauts get into outer space? Circle the picture.*

8.

*Look at number **nine**. Where can astronauts fly in the spacecraft? Circle the picture.*

9.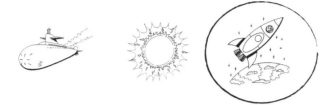

*Look at number **ten**. Where is the solar system? Circle the picture.*

10.

*Look at number **eleven**. What orbits the sun? Circle the picture.*

11.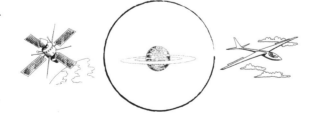

C Read the following directions to the group:

Now I'm going to ask you some more questions about the story. For each question, I'll read four answers. Circle the letter of the correct answer.

*Let's do the **example**. Who goes into outer space?*

*If **astronomers** go into space, circle the letter **a**.*

*If **doctors** go into space, circle the letter **b**.*

*If **teachers** go into space, circle the letter **c**.*

*If **astronauts** go into space, circle the letter **d**.*

Observe students completing the example and assist them as necessary. Then, say:

Astronauts go into space. Did you circle the letter d? *That is the answer.*

Be sure students circle the correct answer.

*Let's do number **twelve**. Why do astronauts need special gear to go into outer space?*

*If it's because **outer space is very dark**, circle the letter **a**.*

*If it's because **there is no oxygen in outer space**, circle the letter **b**.*

*If it's because **there are stars in outer space**, circle the letter **c**.*

*If it's because **there are no people in outer space**, circle the letter **d**.*

*Let's do number **thirteen**. Why is it dangerous to go into outer space?*

*If it's because **astronauts don't like space**, circle the letter **a**.*

*If it's because **a spacecraft cannot go into outer space**, circle the letter **b**.*

*If it's because **many things can go wrong with a spacecraft**, circle the letter **c**.*

*If it's because **the solar system has too many planets**, circle the letter **d**.*

*Let's do number **fourteen**. Why couldn't people fly into outer space before the 1960s?*

*If it's because **they didn't want to**, circle the letter **a**.*

*If it's because **new technologies had to be developed first**, circle the letter **b**.*

*If it's because **there was no time**, circle the letter **c**.*

*If it's because **people were scared of space**, circle the letter **d**.*

Reading

A Read the following directions to the group:

Look at the sentences. A word is missing from each one. Circle the word that completes the sentence.

Now do the **example**.

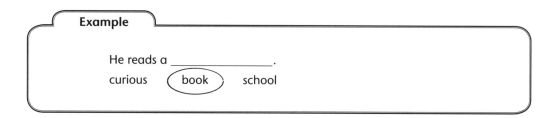

> **Example**
>
> He reads a _____.
> curious   (book)   school

Observe students completing the example and assist them as necessary. Then, say:

Did you circle the second word, book? *That is the word. He reads a* book.

Be sure students circle the correct answer.

Now circle the words for numbers **one** *through* **seven**.

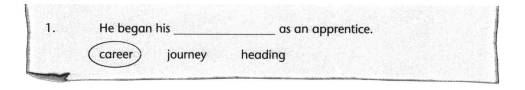

1.   He began his _____ as an apprentice.
     (career)   journey   heading

2.   It is hard to _____ with all this smoke.
     (breathe)   like   be

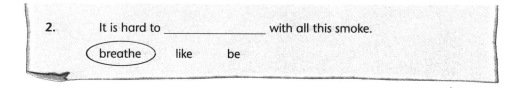

3.   She followed a _____ through the forest.
     mood   horizon   (path)

4. The artist's subject _____ for three hours.

painted   (posed)   pigment

5. They didn't want to _____ driving in the rain.

smell   watch   (risk)

6. The doctor was able to _____ my disease.

(cure)   curious   cured

7. The teacher _____ the attention of the whole class.

determines   styles   (demands)

B Read the following directions to the group:

Read the story. Then, you will answer some questions about it. For each question, circle the correct answer.

> A group of explorers ventured through thick forests. They had read that there was a vast kingdom in this area, but no one knew if the stories were true. So far, their journey had led them through an uncharted wilderness. Sometimes they found trails, but the trails disappeared and led the explorers nowhere. The explorers were discouraged. Then, one day a trail they were following in the forest led them to an ancient temple that rose above the trees. As they entered the temple, the explorers saw mysterious writing on the walls. They saw portraits of ancient emperors. In one room, they found a tomb. In their journals, they recorded all that they saw. They measured the rooms and the pottery that they found in them. They tried to figure out the language written on the walls, but it was different from any language they had seen.

When students have finished reading, ask them to answer the example question.

Example

Who is the story about?

a. An ancient emperor

b. A group of explorers

c. An ancient temple

d. Trails in the forest

Once students have answered the example question, say:

*Did you circle the second answer, "A group of explorers"? That is the correct answer. The story is about a group of explorers. Now answer questions **eight** through **fourteen**.*

8. What were the explorers looking for?

a. Portraits of ancient emperors

b. A vast kingdom

c. Something to write in their journals

d. Ancient pottery

9.   Where were the explorers looking?

    a.   In an ancient cave

    b.   In an ancient map

    c.   In a goddess's tomb

    (d.)   In an uncharted wilderness

10.   What did the writing on the temple walls tell them?

    a.   It told them the age of the temple.

    b.   It told them the names of all the emperors.

    c.   It told them what the temple was used for.

    (d.)   The explorers could not understand the writing.

11.   How did the explorers find the temple?

    a.   By following a guide

    b.   By using a map

    (c.)   By following a trail

    d.   By reading a book

C Allow students additional time to answer questions twelve through fourteen.

12.   Why did the explorers record, in their journals, what they saw?

      (**a.**)   So that they could share their discoveries with others

      b.   So that they could keep the temple a secret

      c.   So that they could build another temple

      d.   So that they could find new treasures

13.   Why did the explorers want to read what was on the walls?

      a.   Because they wanted to find other temples

      b.   Because they wanted to find out where they were in the forest

      (**c.**)   Because they wanted to learn about the people who built the temple

      d.   Because they wanted to build a temple

14.   Why did the explorers have trouble finding the temple?

      a.   Because they lost their maps

      (**b.**)   Because no one knew if it existed

      c.   Because they were looking for new roads

      d.   Because they couldn't read

A Read the following directions to the group:

Look at the example. It is the beginning of a sentence. You will write the rest of the sentence. You can write anything that makes sense to you, as long as it completes the sentence.

Now do the **example**.

> **Example**
>
> When we recycle _____
>
> _____.

Observe students completing the example and assist them as necessary. Then, say:

Did you write something that happens when we recycle? One answer could be "we help protect the environment." The sentence would be "When we recycle, we help protect the environment."

Be sure students understand the directions.

Now finish the sentences for numbers **one** *through* **nine**.

1. The farmer harvests _____

   _____.

2. The movement of _____

   _____.

3. My relationship with _____

   _____.

4. When the suspicious _____

   _____.

5. Fractions are _____

    _____ .

6. What is the benefit _____

    _____ ?

7. I like the vivid _____

    _____ .

8. She painted _____

    _____ .

9. Atoms are _____

    _____ .

B Read the following directions to the group:

You will use the blank lines to write three paragraphs. Each paragraph should be at least three sentences long. Remember to use capital letters and end punctuation.

Now look at the **example***. There are three paragraphs describing a trip into outer space. The first paragraph is about the start of the trip, and says* "The astronaut got into the spacecraft. He waited for the countdown. When the countdown got to zero, he felt the spacecraft shake. He felt the powerful jets push him up into the air. He flew past the clouds. Soon he was in outer space."

The second paragraph is about being in outer space, and says "When the astronaut was in outer space, he floated through the spacecraft. There was no gravity. He looked out the window, and he could see planet Earth very far away. He looked out the other window, and he could see the moon very close."

The third paragraph is about the trip back, and says "It was time to go home. The astronaut was nervous. Reentering Earth's atmosphere is dangerous. The spacecraft started falling toward Earth. It went faster and faster. It started shaking. The astronaut felt a jolt as the spacecraft hit the water. He climbed up and opened the hatch. He looked out over the ocean as he waited for someone to come pick him up."

Example. Write three paragraphs describing a trip into outer space.

> The astronaut got into the spacecraft. He waited for the countdown. When the countdown got to zero, he felt the spacecraft shake. He felt the powerful jets push him up into the air. He flew past the clouds. Soon he was in outer space.
>
> When the astronaut was in outer space, he floated through the spacecraft. There was no gravity. He looked out the window, and he could see planet Earth very far away. He looked out the other window, and he could see the moon very close.
>
> It was time to go home. The astronaut was nervous. Reentering Earth's atmosphere is dangerous. The spacecraft started falling toward Earth. It went faster and faster. It started shaking. The astronaut felt a jolt as the spacecraft hit the water. He climbed up and opened the hatch. He looked out over the ocean as he waited for someone to come pick him up.

Now look at number **ten***. Use the blank lines to write three paragraphs describing a real or an imaginary trip you took.*

10. Write three paragraphs describing a real or an imaginary trip you took.

Administer this assessment individually. Use the Speech Observation Form (Post-Assessment) to record all responses to the questions below.

A Using a copy of the Post-Assessment Images for Speaking (provided at the back of this manual, in the Forms section), ask the student to name each of the images.

1. *What's this?* (Point to a picture.)

Repeat this question for all three images. If the student responds in a language other than English, ask the student to respond in English (*Can you say it in English?*). If the student cannot name at least one item in English, stop and do not ask the rest of the questions.

B Ask the student to explain or describe something about the pictures (in this example, an *office*).

2. *What's an office for?* (or *What do you do in an office?*)

If the student gives a plausible but incorrect response, rephrase the question or ask the student for alternative responses. For instance, if you ask *What do you do in an office?* and the student replies *People go there*, you may ask what people do after they go to an office. If the student is unable to answer, stop and do not ask question 3.

C Ask the student to explain why the function of the item is important.

3. *Why is it important to have a place to work?* (or *Why do we need to have a place to work?*)

If the student responds with a description of the function, ask the question using his or her description. For instance, if the student says *You get stuff done there*, ask why we need a place to get stuff done.

D In this section, prompt the student to repeat the story below. Take notes about the student's version of the story as he or she is telling it.

I'm going to tell you a story. Then, I want you to tell me the same story.

> *Ana wanted to explore her community, so she went outside and started walking down the street. As Ana was walking, she saw a man working in his yard. Ana asked what he was doing. He said he was harvesting squash from his garden. Ana kept walking. Next, she saw a woman getting into her car. Ana asked where the woman was going. She said that she was going to work. Ana asked where she worked. The woman said she worked at the grocery store. Ana kept walking. Next, Ana saw some boys playing. She asked them what they were playing. The boys said they were playing soccer. They asked Ana if she wanted to play. Ana replied, "No, thanks. It's getting late. I have to go home." When Ana got home, her dad was making dinner. She couldn't wait to tell him about all the people she had met.*

Now you tell me the story.

Scoring

In the **Listening and Reading** sections of the Unit Assessments, correct responses to items 1–4 are worth 1 point each, items 5–7 are worth 2 points each, and items 8–9 are worth 5 points each. All items are either correct or incorrect.

In the **Writing** section, items 1–4 are scored correct or incorrect. Each of these items is worth 2 points. Item 5 (multiparagraph writing) is scored using a 3-level rubric, found on pages XXII and XXIII of this manual. If the response scores a level one on the rubric, 4 points are given for the item; if it scores a level two, 8 points are given; if it scores a level three, 12 points are given.

In the **Speaking** section, items 1–5 are scored correct or incorrect using the rubric on pages XXIV and XXV of this manual. A correct response to items 1–3 is worth 2 points; item 4 is worth 6 points; item 5 is worth 8 points.

UNIT ASSESSMENTS

Section		Item(s)	Item Point Values	Scoring Method
Listening	A	1–4	1	Answer Key (correct/incorrect)
	B	5–7	2	Answer Key (correct/incorrect)
	C	8–9	5	Answer Key (correct/incorrect)
Reading	A	1–4	1	Answer Key (correct/incorrect)
	B	5–7	2	Answer Key (correct/incorrect)
	C	8–9	5	Answer Key (correct/incorrect)
Writing	A	1–4	2	Rubric (correct/incorrect)
	B	5	4, 8, or 12	Rubric (3 levels)
Speaking	A	1–3	2	Rubric (correct/incorrect)
	B	4	6	Rubric (correct/incorrect)
	C	5	8	Rubric (correct/incorrect)

Use the table below to convert the numerical scores into proficiency levels.

SECTION SCORE to LEVEL CONVERSION

Unit Assessment	Level
0–6	Beginning
7–14	Intermediate
15–20	Advanced

Point Values (Pre- and Post-Assessments)

In the Listening and Reading sections of the Pre- and Post-Assessments, correct responses to items 1–7 are worth 1 point each, items 8–11 are worth 2 points each, and items 12–14 are worth 5 points each. All items are either correct or incorrect.

In the Writing section, items 1–9 are scored correct or incorrect. Each of these items is worth 2 points. Item 10 (multiparagraph writing) is scored using a 3-level rubric, found on pages XXII and XXIII of this manual. If the response scores a level one on the rubric, 4 points are given for the item; if it scores a level two, 8 points are given; if it scores a level three, 12 points are given.

In the Speaking section, items 1–5 are scored correct or incorrect using the rubric on pages XXIV and XXV of this manual. A correct response to items 1–3 (question 1) is worth 2 points; item 4 (question 2) is worth 6 points; and item 5 (question 3) is worth 8 points. Item 6 (story retelling) is scored on a 3-level rubric worth up to 10 points.

PRE- and POST–ASSESSMENTS

Section		Item(s)	Item Point Values	Scoring Method
Listening	A	1–7	1	Answer Key (correct/incorrect)
	B	8–11	2	Answer Key (correct/incorrect)
	C	12–14	5	Answer Key (correct/incorrect)
Reading	A	1–7	1	Answer Key (correct/incorrect)
	B	8–11	2	Answer Key (correct/incorrect)
	C	12–14	5	Answer Key (correct/incorrect)
Writing	A	1–9	2	Rubric (correct/incorrect)
	B	10	4, 8, or 12	Rubric (3 levels)
Speaking	A	1–3	2	Rubric (correct/incorrect)
	B	4	6	Rubric (correct/incorrect)
	C	5	8	Rubric (correct/incorrect)
	D	6	3, 6, or 10	Rubric (3 levels)

Use the table below to convert the numerical scores into proficiency levels.

SECTION SCORE to LEVEL CONVERSION

Pre- and Post-Assessments	Level
0–9	Beginning
10–21	Intermediate
22–30	Advanced

WRITING PART A

Incorrect

Response is not a comprehensible English sentence. Thus a correct response in another language, an incomprehensible response, or an incomplete English response is incorrect.

Examples:

The cold front <u>freez</u>   .

Her mom encourages her <u>mom</u>   .

The rhythm of the <u>cancion</u>   .

This is a risky <u>wen tha polis</u>   .

Correct

Response is a comprehensible English sentence. There may be errors in grammar and spelling, but the point of the sentence is clear, and the response continues where the stimulus left off.

Examples:

The cold front <u>mad it cold</u>   .

Her mom encourages her <u>do the homwerk</u>   .

The rhythm of the <u>song was pretty</u>   .

This is a risky <u>way to get out</u>   .

WRITING PART B

Write three paragraphs that tell a real or made-up story about a weather event.	Write three paragraphs informing the reader about a natural or human-made wonder of the world.	Write three paragraphs persuading farmers to help protect the environment.
Example 1	Example 2	Example 3

Note: Sample responses refer to the example stimuli above, which are taken from Units 1, 2, and 3 of the *Spotlight Assessments*.

Score 0

Response is illegible or written in another language.

Example 1: *Hay mucha lluvia en el invierno.*
Example 2: *the*
Example 3: *wh*

Score 4 (Level 1)

Response contains at least one word, clause, or phrase that relates to the prompt, but is not a complete sentence (which would be scored at Level 2). It may contain sentences in another language, but only comprehensible English words are given credit. Spelling and punctuation do not need to be correct.

Example 1: *sunnny*
Example 2: *the big waterfal*
Example 3: *Use compos to fertilis.*

Score 8 (Level 2)

Response includes at least one complete, coherent English sentence that is relevant to the prompt. This level includes more elaborate writing that must be related to the prompt. Response may contain systematic errors. This score is also given to three-paragraph responses, if there are systematic errors or incomprehensible words.

Example 1: *ther is rain a lot.*
Example 2: *I seen the gran canon. its reel big and you can down in ther.*
Example 3: *Is good to protect. is good for the envairoment, and good for peopel.*
Farmers culd use organic to fetlais. They culd also use no pest.
In farm meny farmer teik care of the envairoment cos it is importan to prtect the plant an the people.

Score 12 (Level 3)

Response is complete, coherent, and somewhat related to the prompt. It must include three distinct paragraphs. Paragraphs may contain errors in punctuation, spelling, and grammar, as long as there is not a pattern of errors, or errors that would not be made by a native speaker at this age.

Example 1: *There difrent kinds of weather where I live. It depending on the month and the day. One day it is cold, one day it is hot. Today is not hot or cold.*

Today I war a tshirt and some jeens. I seen some other kids warin sandals, but I got snickers. its kinda windy.

Wen its nice like this it is good to be in the sun. My family has a cook in the yard. Some frends come and we have burgers. I like to have a coke with it. then we play soccer in the park.

Example 2: *Ther is a statue call the statue of Liberty. It is in new york. I never been there. But seen some pictures. It is by the water. some peeple look at it from the boat.*

This statue is very tall. It is taller than any house. It is taller than the school. But if you want to you go up inside it. Lotsa people do that. It's a statue of a lady. She got a dres on and she holds a torch. She got a hat that look funny. I don't know what kinda hat that is.

People go there to look at her and go up. Some people just look at her from the boat. Also I think you can by some pictures of her there. Some people like to take there on pictures with a camra.

Example 3: *It is importan to protect the envairronment. When farmers care for the envaironment, they help protect people's health. They also help protect the earth.*

Farmers can protect the envairronment by growing organic products. Organic products are grown with natural fertilisers to make the plants grow strong. They are also grown without pesticides that polute the water and the soil.

When farmers show that they care about us, we want to buy more food from them. I tell my mom to buy food from farmers that like to protect the envaironment. Thats another reason why it is good for farmers to help protect the envaironment.

Separate Domains Assessment Rubrics

SPEAKING PART A

Incorrect	Score 0

Response is not the correct English name of the object or image. Thus a correct response in another language, an incomprehensible response, or an inappropriate English response is incorrect.

Correct	Score 2

Response is the standard English name for the object or image. Response may have a non-English accent or nonstandard pronunciation, but is comprehensible to native English-speakers.

SPEAKING PART B

Incorrect	Score 0

Response is not a standard English phrase or verb describing the image. Thus a correct response in another language, an incomprehensible response, or an inappropriate English response is incorrect.

Examples:
Teacher: *What's the weather like in this picture?*
Student: *Picture.*

Teacher: *What's this pyramid for?*
Student: *Build good.*

Correct	Score 6

Response is a standard English description of the image. Response may have a non-English accent or nonstandard pronunciation, but is comprehensible to native English–speakers. The response needs to include a verb.

Teacher: *What's the old man doing?*
Student: *Speak.*

Teacher: *What's the farmer doing?*
Student: *He plants seeds.*

Teacher: *What's this pyramid for?*
Student: *To show what foods are healthy.*

SPEAKING PART C

Incorrect	Score 0

Response is not a standard English sentence answering the question. Thus a correct response in another language, an incomprehensible response, or an inappropriate English response is incorrect. Because you are asking the student to make inferences, a description of the item is incorrect.

Examples:
Teacher: *Why is the food pyramid important?*
Student: *It is a triangle.*

Teacher: *Why do we wear warm clothes?*
Student: *They warm.*

Teacher: *Why is the farmer putting his harvest into the barn?*
Student: *He's moving his harvest.*

Correct	Score 8

Response is a standard English sentence answering the question. Response may have a non-English accent or nonstandard pronunciation, but is comprehensible to native English-speakers.

Examples:
Teacher: *Why is the food pyramid important?*
Student: *So you can remember to eat healthy foods.*

Teacher: *Why do we wear warm clothes?*
Student: *Cause we don't want to be cold.*

Teacher: *Why is the farmer putting his harvest into the barn?*
Student: *So the animals have something to eat during the winter.*

SPEAKING PART D (Pre- and Post-Assessments Only)

The examples are based on the following story (from the Pre-Assessment) as a stimulus:

John wanted to plant a flower. First, he made a hole in the soil. Next, he put a seed into the hole. Then, he filled the hole with soil. But he wasn't done yet. He had to water the seed every day. For many days, John waited to see the flower. Then, one day he went out to water the plant, and he saw two tiny leaves coming up out of the soil. John kept watering the plant every day. Every day the plant got taller, the stem got thicker, and the leaves grew. Soon the flower started to grow at the top. Then, one day, when John went out to water his flower, the petals had opened. It was beautiful! John was so happy that he had cared for his plant and had waited patiently for the flower to bloom.

Score 0

Response ranges from no comprehensible English response to isolated English words that may or may not relate to the story. It may be incomprehensible or in another language.

Example 1: *John pone la semilla en la tierra.*
Example 2: *What happen?*
Example 3: *Growing.*

Score 3 (Level 1)

Response is an English phrase, clause, or sentence(s) unconnected to a narrative.

Example 1: *He plant a flower.*
Example 2: *John put a seed in the ground. A flower grow.*
Example 3: *John happy. John grow a flower. He water all the time.*

Score 6 (Level 2)

Response is a story with a beginning, a middle, and an end, but with a pattern of significant errors. It clearly contains more significant errors than a native speaker would produce.

Example 1: *John dig a hole. He put a seed in there. He water it so it grows. A flower come up. He is so happy he has a flower.*
Example 2: *The story's about a guy name John. He dig a hole. He put a seed in there. The seed grow. John put water on the hole. Then there a flower. That's all.*
Example 3: *This guy put a seed in a hole. He put dirt in there. Some leaves comin'. There's a plant with a flower on it. He's happy about that.*

Score 10 (Level 3)

Response is a story with a beginning, a middle, and an end, with occasional minor errors. Sounds like a native English-speaker, though perhaps with a limited vocabulary.

Example 1: *Okay, there's a guy named John. He's got a seed, and he wants to grow a flower. So he digs a hole. And he puts a seed in there. Then, he covers it up with dirt. Now he waters it all the time. He waits but nothin' happens. But he keeps giving it water. Then, one day he sees some leaves. And then later he sees a stem. The plant grows and grows. It gets big. Then the flower opens, and John's real happy. Because he's the one who made it grow there.*

Example 2: *Well the boy named John wants to grow a flower. He knows what he's gotta do. He plants it in the ground. He covers it up. And then he waters it every day. At first it don't grow. And I think he's worried or sad there's no flower. But he keeps giving water anyway. So one day he sees some leaves there. And he gives it more water every day. The leaves get bigger and bigger and bigger. The plant gets tall. And then the flower opens. John is so happy.*

Example 3: *This is a story about a man that growed a flower. All he had was a little seed. Then, he put it in a hole. And every day he give some water to it. The seed drink up that water. But it is in the ground and the man John can't see it. One day the leaf comes up. Now he knows this plant is growin'. But he still gotta give it more water. Now he can watch it grow all the time. The stem get thick and the leaf get big. It grows real big. Then, he see the flower open up. Boy that made him happy.*

The following chart can be used to quickly understand the meaning of assessment results, and to plan instruction. It can also be helpful for explaining student abilities and progress to parents and administrators.

INTERPRETATION OF SEPARATE DOMAINS ASSESSMENT LEVELS

	Beginning	Intermediate	Advanced
Listening	Ranges from initial learner to understanding of some isolated words, and occasionally comprehends short, clear sentences.	Ranges from general grasp of many isolated words to understanding simple sentences and grammatical structures.	Ranges from usually understanding sentences about familiar topics to near-fluency; can often infer meaning of unknown words.
Speaking	Ranges from no speech skills to ability to name familiar objects.	Ability to describe behaviors, actions, or functions of a given object in phrases or simple sentences.	Ability to compare and contrast familiar objects, with some level of abstraction; generally able to speak in complete, often complex sentences.
Reading	Ranges from illiteracy to ability to derive limited meaning through recognition of words and phrases.	Ranges from ability to understand some details of most simple written statements to comprehension of main ideas and some key details.	Ranges from ability to generally understand main ideas and many details in simple texts to near-fluency.
Writing	Ranges from illiteracy to ability to write names of some familiar objects and, occasionally, actions.	Usually able to write appropriate phrases and clauses, and can often write complete sentences.	Able to write complete, coherent sentences that are appropriate to the situation. Can write paragraphs with some errors in grammar and punctuation.

Beginning Level

Comprehension

- Student requires visual or tactile cues for comprehension, but sometimes misinterprets them
- Student may misinterpret nonverbal communication (e.g., gestures and facial expressions)
- Verbal communication requires contextual clues for student to understand message
- Student needs repetition and/or rephrasing in order to grasp basic meaning of message
- Meaning is lost because of student's lack of familiarity with linguistic structures (e.g., verb tense and word order)
- Student may not distinguish pauses from conclusion of message during communication
- Comprehension of message is enhanced by access to native-language support

Production

- Student primarily uses gestures and body language for communication; in some cases these gestures may be more appropriate to home culture than to American culture
- Student's messages tend to depend on gestures, facial expressions, and other contextual clues
- Student's verbal communications are typically limited to isolated words or memorized phrases (e.g., "good morning")
- Student may be able to repeat words with nativelike pronunciation and intonation, but generally cannot do so spontaneously
- When encountering difficulty communicating, student tends to repeat words and phrases, rather than rephrasing message
- Student may mix words from native language into English messages
- Student lacks ability to convey meaning through grammatical structures (e.g., verb tense and word order)
- Student's response (or lack thereof) is sometimes inappropriate to stimulus

Intermediate Level

Comprehension

- Student comprehends simple communications without visual cues, especially when dealing with familiar topics
- Student makes use of, and often depends on, nonverbal cues to interpret verbal messages
- Student comprehends general ideas of more complex communications, while missing details
- Student's comprehension is limited by unfamiliarity with grammatical structures
- As student increases in proficiency, ability to anticipate (and mis-anticipate) the meaning of messages increases
- Student can accurately interpret the meaning of pauses, including the end of   a message
- Student may occasionally benefit from access to some native-language support

Production

- Student uses some gestures and body language appropriate to American culture
- Student communicates with little dependence on gestures
- Student's communications often include sentences, especially when discussing familiar topics
- Student's pronunciation and intonation patterns allow for communication with teachers or others accustomed to communicating with ESL students
- When encountering difficulty communicating, student modifies and/or rephrases message to enhance comprehension
- Student rarely mixes words from native language into English messages when discussing familiar topics
- As student shifts from repetition of language structures to creative expression, grammatical errors may increase along with ability to convey meaning and express feelings
- Student's responses are generally appropriate to stimulus

Advanced Level

Comprehension

- Student comprehends main ideas and important details on many topics without reliance on contextual clues

- Student correctly interprets nonverbal cues, but does not rely on them to understand message

- Student is able to identify details that need clarification in a message, and to understand the impact of these details on the rest of the message

- Student's comprehension is rarely hindered by unfamiliarity with grammatical structures

- Student is usually able to anticipate the meaning of messages when dealing with familiar topics

- Student can accurately interpret the meaning of pauses, including the end of a message

- Student does not require native-language support

Production

- Student has mastered most gestures and body language used by Americans

- Student does not depend on gestures to communicate

- Student's communications often include connected sentences and paragraphs with a logical progression

- Student's pronunciation and intonation patterns allow for communication with most native speakers

- Student rarely encounters difficulty communicating, unless topic is especially unfamiliar

- Student is able to communicate without using words from native language

- Student self-corrects even when errors do not impede communication

- Student's responses are rarely inappropriate to stimulus

Sample Responses

These notes and writing samples are based on a group paragraph-writing activity.

Student 1 (Production)

Teacher's Notes

- Communicates almost entirely in Eng.
- Can code-switch, tends not to
- Takes lead in completing activity
- Resolves disagreements well
- Helps others with spelling
- Some spelling errors
- Reads work aloud with fluency

Student's Writing Sample

Sara was waching TV. The weather reporter said that a tornado was in her town. She ran to the kichen to tell her dad. Sara's dad already heard about it because he was listening to the radio. They listen to what the reporter tells them to do.

Then Sara's mom gets home. She said it was so windy she could hardly drive. They got a flashlite and a radio with batteries. They covered the windows. They went to the basement.

In the basement they listened to the radio. The radio said the tornado was coming close to the city. It hit some houses. Sara and her parents were scared. Then they heard that the tornado stoped. They went upstairs and everything was fine. The roof was ok and the windows were not broken. They were so happy.

Rating:

Advanced According to the teacher's notes, the student spoke almost entirely in English during the activity, and tended not to switch to another language (code-switch). The student's conflict resolution indicates the ability to communicate his or her own ideas in a give-and-take interaction with others. The willingness to take a leadership role with the activity shows a high degree of confidence in his or her English-writing skills.

Student 2 (Production)

Teacher's Notes

- Relies heavily on first language
- Understands most questions in English
- Stays in present tense
- Very limited English vocabulary
- Cannot describe feelings in English

Student's Writing Sample

lots ov rane com. thar watr al ovr. them cant swim. vary scary.

Rating:

Beginning The student relies heavily on Spanish to communicate thoughts, and can only use very limited English vocabulary. The student did not demonstrate the ability to communicate beyond the present tense. Taken together, these facts place the student at the beginning level of English-language production.

Student 3 (Comprehension)

Teacher's Notes
- Can read isolated English words
- Trouble reading instructions
- Understands verbal descriptions
- Can ask and answer questions in English

Rating:

Intermediate According to the teacher's notes, this student had trouble reading the instructions in English, but was able to understand the project with some discussion. This indicates that the student has developed the ability to comprehend enough English to ask questions and come to a better understanding of textual material. Considering that the student comprehends some written English, and a fair amount of spoken English, his or her comprehension should be rated as Intermediate.

Student 4 (Comprehension)

Teacher's Notes
- Asks questions to clarify
- Understands activity well
- Rephrases directions for partner
- Grammar problems
- Reads questions to partner

Rating:

Advanced According to the teacher's notes, this student is able to understand directions well enough to explain them to a partner. The student also uses written instructions to help explain the activity. The ability to ask questions to clarify meaning also indicates competent comprehension. Grammar problems do not detract from the student's comprehension of both written and spoken English.

Interpreting Results

The following charts can be used to quickly understand the meaning of assessment results, and to plan instruction. They can also be helpful for explaining student abilities and progress to parents and administrators.

INTERPRETATION OF INTEGRATED DOMAINS ASSESSMENT LEVELS

Beginning

Comprehension	Production
Ranges from initial contact with English to learner who comprehends messages depending on visual/tactile cues. Loses meaning owing to lack of knowledge of linguistic structures (e.g., verb tense and word order).	Produces responses ranging from silence to isolated words or memorized phrases. Lacks ability to convey meaning using grammatical structures (e.g., verb tense and word order).

Intermediate

Comprehension	Production
Comprehension limited to familiar topics; depends on nonverbal cues. Understanding impeded by lack of familiarity with grammatical structures.	Produces appropriate responses, including sentences when addressing familiar topics. Grammatical errors may increase along with ability to convey meaning and express feelings.

Advanced

Comprehension	Production
Comprehends main ideas and most details without support from visual aids or contextual cues. Unfamiliar structures rarely impede understanding.	Communicates using connected sentences and paragraphs. Can be understood by most native speakers. Self-corrects even when not necessary.

Forms

Separate Domains Assessment Speech Observation Form (Units 1–8)

Student Name _____ Date _____ Unit _____

Stimuli: _____
(Write names of all stimuli, separated by commas.)

Responses:

1a. _____ 1b. _____ 1c. _____

2. _____

3. _____

- -

Student Name _____ Date _____ Unit _____

Stimuli: _____
(Write names of all stimuli, separated by commas.)

Responses:

1a. _____ 1b. _____ 1c. _____

2. _____

3. _____

- -

Student Name _____ Date _____ Unit _____

Stimuli: _____

(Write names of all stimuli, separated by commas.)

Responses:

1a. _____ 1b. _____ 1c. _____

2. _____

3. _____

Separate Domains Assessment Speech Observation Form (Pre-Assessment)

Student Name _____ Date _____

1. Name (write response on line next to word)

Book _____ Soldier _____ Kitchen _____

2. Explain or describe (write object chosen and response)

Object: _____ Response: _____

3. Explain the function (write object chosen and response)

Object: _____ Response: _____

_____

4. Story Retelling

Response: _____

_____

_____

_____

_____

_____

_____

_____

Separate Domains Assessment Speech Observation Form (Post-Assessment)

Student Name _____ Date _____

1. Name (write response on line next to word)

Car _____ Police officer _____ Office _____

2. Explain or describe (write object chosen and response)

Object: _____ Response: _____

3. Explain the function (write object chosen and response)

Object: _____ Response: _____

_____

4. Story Retelling

Response: _____

_____

_____

_____

_____

_____

_____

_____

Integrated Domains Assessment Observation Form

Comprehension

Student Name _____ Date _____ Unit _____

Comprehension Level: Beginning   Intermediate   Advanced

(Mark appropriate level.)

Observations / Notes: _____

_____

_____

_____

_____

Note: See rubric for scoring "Comprehension."

- -

Integrated Domains Assessment Observation Form

Production

Student Name _____ Date _____ Unit _____

Production Level: Beginning   Intermediate   Advanced

(Mark appropriate level.)

Observations / Notes: _____

_____

_____

_____

_____

Attach student's writing sample to this form.

Note: See rubric for scoring "Production."

Unit _____ Date _____ Teacher _____

Student Name	Integrated Domains		Separate Domains				
	Comp. Level	Prod. Level	Listening	Reading	Writing	Speaking	Total
1							
2							
3							
4							
5							
6							
7							
8							
9							
10							
11							
12							
13							
14							
15							
16							
17							
18							
19							
20							
21							
22							
23							
24							
25							

Student Name _____

Teacher Name _____

		Separate Domains								
Integrated Domains		Listening		Reading		Writing		Speaking		Total
Comp. Level	Prod. Level	Score	Level	Score	Level	Score	Level	Score	Level	Score	Level
Unit										
Pre										
1										
2										
3										
4										
5										
6										
7										
8										
Post										